MICHAEL HENRY

Old-growth Forest Walks

26 HIKES IN ONTARIO'S GREENBELT

Fitzhenry & Whiteside

Published in Canada by Fitzhenry & Whiteside Limited,
209 Wicksteed Avenue, Unit 51, Toronto, ON M4G 0B1

Published in the United States by Fitzhenry & Whiteside Limited,
60 Leo Birmingham Pkwy, Ste 107, Brighton, MA 02135

Fitzhenry & Whiteside Limited acknowledges with thanks the Canada Council for the Arts and the Ontario Arts Council for their support of our publishing program. We acknowledge the financial support of the Government of Canada through the Canada Book Fund (CBF) for our publishing activities.

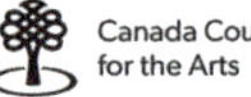

Library and Archives Canada Cataloguing in Publication
Title: Old-growth forest walks : 26 hikes in Ontario's Greenbelt / Michael Henry.
Names: Henry, Michael, 1972- author
Identifiers: Canadiana 20240421167 | ISBN 9781554556472 (softcover)
Subjects: LCSH: Old growth forests—Ontario, Southern—Guidebooks. | LCSH: Walking—Ontario, Southern—
Guidebooks. | LCSH: Ontario, Southern—Guidebooks. | LCGFT: Guidebooks.
Classification: LCC QH106.2.O5 H43 2024 | DDC 578.7309713—dc23

Publisher Cataloging-in-Publication Data (U.S.)
Names: Henry, Michael, 1972- author.
Title: Old-growth forest walks : 26 hikes in Ontario's Greenbelt / Michael Henry.
Description: Toronto, Ontario : Fitzhenry & Whiteside, 2024. | Summary: Provides a physical and historical description of the variety of old-growth forests in Southern Ontario's Greenbelt region, and details the many hiking trails that wend their way through it.
Identifiers: ISBN 978-1-55455-647-2 (paperback)
Subjects: LCSH: Old growth forests – Ontario, Southern -- Guidebooks. | Greenbelts – Ontario, Southern – Guidebooks. | Walking – Ontario, Southern – Guidebooks. | Ontario, Southern – Guidebooks. | Ontario, Southern – History. |BISAC: NATURE / Ecosystems & Habitats / Forests & Rainforests.| NATURE / Plants / Trees. | TRAVEL / Canada / Ontario (ON) | TRAVEL / Special Interest / Hikes & Walks.
Classification: LCC F1057.7.H5212 OL44 2024 | DDC 917.13 – dc23

Cover and interior design by Tanya Montini
Printed in Canada by Copywell

Possibility grows here.

Fitzhenry & Whiteside Limited

This book is dedicated to the generations of people who will come after us and all the species we coexist with, for whom we act as stewards of this planet. Also to family and friends who bring beauty and meaning to the world. And finally to the species that we have lost, like the passenger pigeon, that have left the world a little bit impoverished.

Lake Huron (Georgian Bay)
Ontario
Forested Area
Bruce Trail
Niagara
Escarpment
Lake Simcoe
Ontario's Greenbelt
Oak Ridges Moraine
Greenbelt Cycle Route
Oak Ridges Trail
Escarpment
Lake Erie
Lake Ontario
U.S.A.
N
0 25 50 km
1
2
3
4
5
6
7
8
9
10
11
12
13
14
15
16
17
18
19
20
21
22
23
24
25
26

Acknowledgments

I'd like to extend a big thank you to the many people who helped make this book a reality by sharing knowledge, reviewing the text, and more, including (but not limited to): Phil Abbot; Ian Attridge; Jennifer Bonnell; Eric Davies; James Garrat; Allison Hands; Ian Jackson; Aniko, Elena and Lev Kiriloff; Doug Larson; Thomas Lee; Bruce Mackenzie; Paul O'Hara; Peter Quinby; Amy Quinn; Karen Reynolds-Drew; Cameron Richardson; Stephen Smith; Wayne Terryberry; Nate Torenvliet; and Steve Varga.

This book began as a project of Ancient Forest Exploration and Research, with funding provided by the Greenbelt Foundation.

Photos by Michael Henry unless otherwise credited.

Table of Contents

Introduction

When I set out to visit the old-growth forests of the Greenbelt, I expected to be wowed by the trees—after all, Ontario's oldest tree is in the Greenbelt, a 1300-year-old white cedar growing on a cliff at Lion's Head. And Peter's Woods, at the eastern edge of the Greenbelt, is one of very few forests in southern Ontario that was never logged and boasts trees over 400-years-old. What I didn't anticipate was being so fascinated by the human history that happened alongside the trees.

Many stories of First Nations, the settlement of Upper Canada, and then the Province of Ontario are woven through this book because the trees witnessed them, and forests often survived because of some historical idiosyncrasy. In the pages to come, you'll join me on this journey through some of southern Ontario's most impressive forests. If you live in the GTA, they may be closer than you realize. But let's set the stage with a short history of the Greenbelt.

THE MAKING OF ONTARIO'S GREENBELT

Ontario's Greenbelt began as lines on a map that were the collective creation of citizens, scientists, First Nations, governments of all Ontario's political

Terrace Creek Falls is one of dozens of waterfalls captured within the Greenbelt.

parties, and the land itself. The concept was decades in the making. Today it is an area of mixed land use and limited development that circles the GTA like a crown, with a spur that runs up the Niagara Escarpment to the tip of the Bruce Peninsula. It also includes major river valleys that drain through the GTA. The Greenbelt's goals of conserving nature and limiting sprawl are immensely popular in Ontario: polling in 2020 found that most Ontarians support the Greenbelt, and 84% said they consider the Greenbelt a "source of pride."

The Greenbelt puts a stopper on seemingly limitless urban sprawl, and it includes many of Southern Ontario's most ecologically rich natural areas—including many old-growth forests running the gamut from dwarf ancient cedars on cliffs, to open oak savannah and shady maple forest. The Greenbelt boasts some of Ontario's most iconic long-distance hiking trails, including the Bruce Trail, Oak Ridges Trail, and the Humber Valley Heritage Trail. All three of these wind their way through old-growth forests at some point.

But when I think of the Greenbelt, what I think of are moments. Like the first time I stumbled on a dramatic lookout over Duffins Creek valley across forests and farms on the Seaton Trail in Pickering. The moment when, leaning on an oak tree near Niagara-on-the-Lake, I realized there could be musket balls from 1812 embedded deep within. Or hiking the rocky limestone terraces of the Bruce Trail, finding waterfalls and dramatic views a stone's throw from Canada's most densely populated urban landscapes. The list continues, of course, throughout the pages of this book.

Ontario's Greenbelt is said to be the largest of its kind in the world, part of a global movement 100 years in the making. In Ontario, it began with the Niagara Escarpment, the Oak Ridges Moraine, and Hurricane Hazel.

THE NIAGARA ESCARPMENT

The Niagara Escarpment reveals itself in the plummet of Niagara Falls, in dramatic white cliffs visible from Highway 401 and the QEW, or limestone shelves where the Bruce Peninsula abruptly meets the aquamarine waters of Georgian Bay. Ontarians think of it as ours, but we actually share it with New York State, Michigan, and Wisconsin, as it defines a large arc around three great lakes: Ontario, Huron, and Michigan. The Limestone of the escarpment was laid down in a shallow tropical sea over 400 million years ago, at a time when ocean life was flourishing and rapidly evolving, and terrestrial life was just beginning. Fossils of primitive fish, invertebrates, corals, and aquatic plants offer a look at the rich history of life on earth, and some areas of the Escarpment rank among Canada's most important sites for fossils.

The cliffs of the escarpment were not formed by movement at a fault line, but rather by differential erosion. That may need some explanation. The dolomitic limestone that makes up the escarpment is harder than the shale that is beneath it, so the shale weathers much more quickly, causing the limestone to appear to rise up and form cliffs over millions of years. At the top of the cliff, the escarpment angles away from the cliff edge and disappears under layers of glacial till and soil, but it is still there, buried. Essentially the cliffs are close to the ancient shorelines of the sea, the limestone slopes down under what was once the waters of the ocean but has since filled in with layers of rock laid down over the following 150 million years, or soil deposited by glaciers over the past two million years. Most of Lake Huron, Lake Erie, and Lake Michigan are contained within the basin of the ancient sea, their outer shorelines often roughly matching the shoreline during the Silurian period 420 million years ago.

During settlement, the Niagara Escarpment was largely viewed as an obstacle, or sometimes as a good location for a water-powered mill. Farm fields ended where the bedrock came close to the surface at varying distances from the cliff edge. This and the steep forested slopes below the escarpment combined to create a natural forest corridor within a highly

The Niagara Escarpment meets Georgian Bay on the Bruce Peninsula.

managed landscape, but with little formal protection. That was the case up to the 1960s.

On September 23, 1960, an unlikely group of four people gathered in a home in Hamilton, Ontario: Philip Gosling, a real estate agent; Ray Lowes, a metallurgist; Robert MacLaren, president of the Hamilton Naturalists; and Norman Pearson, a professor and city planner for Burlington. Their goal was to begin planning "the Appalachian Trail of Ontario," which would meander from Niagara Falls to Tobermory, following the Niagara Escarpment. They agreed to call it the Bruce Trail since it would lead to the Bruce Peninsula, and it was a short catchy name that would fit comfortably on signs. From the start, it was a pragmatic group, but with a grand vision. And it would succeed,—despite the necessity of patching together a network of public and private land into a single trail. A decade later, a dozen people had hiked the trail end to end, and thousands of people who had hiked portions of it were beginning to take it for granted. As co-founder, Ray Lowes, would write in 1970, "The Bruce Trail is not just a pleasant path across the country; it is a powerful argument, merely because it exists, and is used, for the value of wilderness and a natural environment. It is an argument for setting aside significant sections of unique environment for the physical and mental health of Canadians."

A lot had happened in the intervening decade, and Lowes's comments reflected a new reality, which arguably the Bruce Trail played a role in shaping. In 1962, a quarry just off highway 401 in Milton blasted a very public hole in the escarpment, within view of Highway 401. Even though much of the aggregate from the quarry would be used for expansion of the highway, drivers didn't like to be reminded that the Niagara Escarpment, a ribbon of green across southern Ontario, had little protection from development. This quarry is often credited with catalyzing the movement to protect the Escarpment.

The Bruce Trail south of Scotsdale Farm

On the 10th of March 1967, John Robarts, Premier of Ontario, announced "a wide ranging study of the Niagara Escarpment with a view to preserving its entire length—as a recreation area for the people of Ontario." The resulting study was finalized in 1969 and proposed a hierarchy of land use in which the most ecologically or historically significant areas would be acquired outright and preserved as parkland; another segment would be protected through private land easements; and the remainder would receive some regulatory protection to limit the type and extent of development that could occur. Amazingly, the broad elements of the plan and many of the details were accepted and incorporated into the *Niagara Escarpment Planning and Development Act* in 1973, and the Niagara Escarpment Plan in 1985.

In 1990, the Niagara Escarpment was designated as a UNESCO World Biosphere Reserve, the sixth to be designated in Canada. At the time of writing, there are 727 biosphere reserves designated globally, 18 of which are in Canada. The designation is a good fit. Biosphere reserves are meant to identify the world's most important ecosystems, and offer a mosaic of conservation in three zones: strictly protected core areas, buffer zones, and a transition area where sustainable development may occur. The Niagara Escarpment Plan predated UNESCO's Man and Biosphere Program, but foreshadowed it almost perfectly.

However, as Sandra Patano and L. Anders Sandberg explain in a 2005 analysis, the *Niagara Escarpment Planning and Development Act* is "a development measure that treats protection as a constraint rather than a priority to development and the NEC approves more than 90 percent of all development applications." Unfortunately, there's no plan in place to track the decisions and evaluate how well they conform to the Niagara Escarpment Plan, or the larger goal of sustainable development.

Like the rest of the Greenbelt, the Niagara Escarpment Plan is a work in progress. But its success is evident to the roughly 400,000 people who

Rock cap fern is found on limestone boulders along the Niagara Escarpment.

hike the trail each year, past waterfalls, historic towns, and dramatic views with hawks wheeling on updrafts. The shallow soils and steep valleys of the escarpment naturally protected some of the forests along its length; 10 of the old-growth forests in this book are in the area regulated by the Niagara Escarpment Plan, and many others were omitted due to poor access but are equally valuable.

For example, Ontario's oldest trees (over 1300-years-old) are found on the cliffs at Lion's Head, but I decided to leave it out of this book. The trails at Lion's Head run along the top of the escarpment, offering beautiful views of Georgian Bay but only glimpses of ancient cedars. The cedars are somewhat younger at Rattlesnake Point and Flowerpot Island, but the opportunities to get a look at them are much better, so they are included.

When the Greenbelt was created in 2005, the Niagara Escarpment was integrated into it, though development continues to be regulated under the Niagara Escarpment Plan in addition to the Greenbelt Plan.

THE OAK RIDGES MORAINE

Around 15,000 years ago, as the massive kilometres-thick ice sheets of the Wisconsin glacial period were receding, a long narrow lake formed between two lobes of ice. It was only about 13 km wide, but it stretched about 160 km, from present-day Rice Lake to the Niagara Escarpment. It paralleled the north shore of Lake Ontario, covering (not coincidentally) roughly the same area as the Oak Ridges Moraine does today. Glacial rivers carried in vast amounts of sediment, which settled out in layers. Finally, centuries later, this lake drained through a channel where Campbellford is found today. After it drained, where there had once been a lake, a hill was left behind, composed of layers of sediment.

At various times during the formation of the Moraine, glaciers dropped unsorted glacial till (a mix of stones, sand, silt, and clay all jumbled together) on top of the sand and gravel layers, building the hill higher and creating a complex of relatively permeable and impermeable layers. Taken together, these create aquifers, large underground reservoirs that store water from rain or melting snow and gradually release it. Rainwater readily percolates into and through the upper layers of the Moraine, but it slows down and flows sideways when it hits layers rich in clay and silt.

Altogether, geologists have defined three aquifers: the upper, middle, and lower. Rainwater readily soaks into the surface of the moraine; a majority travels through the upper aquifer and is mostly released into the headwater streams in the GTA. Some percolates further into the lower aquifers and is released to streams and lakes further away. To give a

Seepage from the Oak Ridges Moraine supports ferns and horsetails.

sense of the vast amounts of water that travel through the aquifers, in the headwaters of Duffins Creek and West Duffins Creek alone, 1400 litres of water are absorbed into the ground every second (averaged year-round). A lot of it percolates into the ground during big rainfalls—this helps reduce flooding and stabilize stream flows throughout the year. Knowing this, it's not hard to see that paving large tracts of the Moraine might be a bad idea.

The Oak Ridges Moraine has always been a distinctive feature since the last ice age, and would have been familiar to First Nations over the thousands of years that they lived here. Among other things, it was a barrier to travel, and many of the historic portage trails that defined travel in Southern Ontario were designed to either cross or bypass the Moraine—

one of the most famous being the Carrying Place Trail that followed the Humber River, the only watercourse that cuts right through the Oak Ridges Moraine. Hunting and gathering on the moraine were common, permanent Indigenous settlements probably less so.

Following colonial settlement, the height of land known as Oak Ridge was noted as early as 1829 by J.J. Bigsby, and it had been more formally defined as the Oak Ridges Moraine by 1913. It remained a barrier of sorts, a thinly settled height of land north of what was quickly becoming one of Canada's most densely populated areas. But the same things that made it a barrier to settlement also made it a movement corridor for wildlife, and the "rain barrel of southern Ontario."

The politics of the Moraine started coming to a head in the 1980s. Suburbs were starting to leapfrog onto the Moraine because land was cheap and the views were good. Citizens were organizing on a local level to fight haphazard development, but they tended to lose local planning battles. In the late 80s, two graduate students living in Peterborough, Don Alexander and John Fisher, were among the first to frame local development issues in the context of the broader Oak Ridges Moraine.

Don Alexander started a PhD in Waterloo, while still living in Peterborough. His commute sometimes took him along the ridge of the moraine. When you drive across the north-south axis of the Moraine, your ears might pop as you gain elevation, but it's easy to overlook its significance, since it averages only 13 km wide and you're quickly across it. Drive it lengthwise, which takes several hours, and you're clearly on a major feature of southern Ontario.

Alexander described this to his friend, John Fisher, a master's student at Trent University with an interest in natural heritage system planning, and the two of them started doing some research. They figured out that this relatively undeveloped hilly landscape Alexander was commuting

Trees in Peter's Woods, at the east end of the Oak Ridges Moraine, reach over 400-years-old.

through was called the Oak Ridges Moraine, and as Fisher drew in the watersheds flowing from it by hand (there are at least 22 major watersheds with headwaters on the Moraine), they began to see what the case for its protection might look like.

The two friends presented under the banner Save the Oak Ridges Moraine (S.T.O.R.M.) for the first time at a public hearing in Ganaraska, where a group of local citizens was fighting a housing development. When Dorothy Izzard in King City read about it in the paper, she knew she had to give Alexander and Fisher a call—she was chairing a committee that was also called Save the Oak Ridges Moraine (STORM), which was part of Concerned Citizens of King Township.

In 1990, the merged "STORM coalition" was incorporated as a not-for-profit organization that would rapidly grow into an umbrella organization for at least 30 groups that had formerly been waging lonely voice-in-the-wilderness-style battles over development on the Moraine. Individually, it was almost impossible to win against the powerful home-builder companies, but collectively they had power.

The idea of the Oak Ridges Moraine as a protected landscape was first recognized by a Liberal provincial government in the late 1980s. It was studied and developed by the subsequent NDP government in the early 1990s, before being shelved by the newly elected Harris Conservative government, which had deep ties to housing developers. Years later, the same Conservative government yielded to public pressure and ultimately protected the Moraine.

It has been recognized for decades that the Moraine functions as a conservation corridor for the movement of animals and migration of plants, etc., and its connections to the escarpment, as well as the Algonquin to Adirondack corridor, were part of the case for its protection from the beginning. So, it's no surprise that one of the things that catalyzed the

Walkers on a section of the Oak Ridges Moraine Trail

movement at the turn of the millennium was proposed development in Richmond Hill that would have built homes on one of the narrowest points of the Moraine, effectively cutting it in two. On a bitterly cold February night, 1500 people showed up to a council meeting, forcing them to relocate from council chambers to the ballroom of a nearby hotel. The meeting went on until midnight, with one concerned citizen after another speaking against the amendment to the town's official plan.

Defenders of the Moraine won the night, but the decision was immediately appealed to the Ontario Municipal Board—a process that had become even more tilted toward developers (over 70% of natural heritage cases at the Ontario Municipal Board were decided in favour of developers). Ultimately, after a lot of bad press, and losing a by-election, the Conservative government changed course and the *Oak Ridges Moraine Conservation Act* was passed in 2001 with unanimous three-party approval. In a final twist, however, the Minister of Municipal Affairs and Housing, Chris Hodgson, used a zoning order to allow 6600 houses to be built on the disputed land in Richmond Hill, ultimately splitting the Moraine in two.

FLOODPLAINS AND AIRPORT LANDS

One of the defining moments of Ontario Conservation was the arrival of Hurricane Hazel in 1954, during which 28cm of rain fell in less than two days, 81 people died, and 3000 were left homeless by flooding. This led to a great rethinking of development in floodplains, the expansion of Ontario's conservation authorities, and the expropriation of large tracts of land that were considered vulnerable to flooding.

Toronto would be forever after a city with wide swatches of green running through it, particularly along the Humber, Don, and Rouge River valleys. It's a character we've come to accept as though it were inevitable, but without a freak (less than once-a-century) storm during Toronto's

The Seaton Trail runs along the edge of the protected Duffins Rouge Agricultural Preserve. The farm fields and forests behind this sign are owned by a property developer who nearly succeeded in having the protection removed.

formative years, the city might have developed very differently.

Fast forward to 1972, when the Government of Canada expropriated 75 sq km of land on the boundary of Pickering and Scarborough (known as the Pickering Lands) to develop a new airport. By 1975, the airport was put on hold indefinitely, but the federal government held on to the lands, leasing them back to residential, farm, and commercial tenants. The province also expropriated land at the time, known as the Seaton Lands. For decades, the combined public land was an informal greenbelt of its own, an area of mixed-use and low development while the city grew up around it.

Significant parts of Rouge Park, and the area around the Seaton Trail, owe their existence to these expropriations. In the end, about half the Seaton Lands to the east of Duffins Creek were made available for development, the remainder protected as greenspace, mostly outside of the Greenbelt. Some of the land owned by developers on the Oak Ridges Moraine was exchanged for the Seaton Lands east of the Creek. I'm not sure this was a good trade, since water quality of the healthiest streams left in the GTA is imperilled by the development.

The portion of the Seaton Lands to the west of the creek became the Duffins Rouge Agricultural Preserve in 2005, to be protected in multiple ways from development in perpetuity. Or until 2022, when Doug Ford's Conservative government briefly stripped it from the Greenbelt. Wealthy developers had bought the farmland for as little as $8000 an acre and worked behind the scenes for years to change the zoning. But their victory was transient—the Ford government dramatically reversed the decision in September 2023, after intense pressure from the public, a scathing Auditor General's report, and resignation of two cabinet ministers. The area between the Seaton Trail and Rouge National Urban Park now stands as a testament to the resilience of the Greenbelt.

CANADA'S BEST FARMLAND

We all know that Canada is a huge country, but our intuition will tell us that a lot of that land isn't very suited to growing food. And our intuition would be right! Only 7.3% of Canada is suitable as farmland, due to soils and climate, and only 0.5% is class one land (the highest grade). Most of Canada's prime agricultural land is in Ontario, which is also where the most rapid urban expansion is occurring. As a result, Ontario lost almost 11,000 sq km (2.7 million acres) of productive farmland between 1976 and 2013, almost 20% of the total. In 2021, Ontario was losing 319 acres of farmland every day. It's hard to see how this is sustainable.

Aside from its obvious role of growing food, farmland can provide wildlife and pollinator habitat, sequester carbon (especially in the soil), regulate water and runoff, have aesthetic and cultural value, and create jobs in the agricultural sector. A significant portion of the 1.8 million acres protected by Ontario's Greenbelt is farmland, and one of the goals of the greenbelt is to preserve it under the designation of "protected countryside." But is it working? Is the Greenbelt protecting the farmland within its boundaries—and even if it is, does development simply leapfrog over it to consume as much or even more farmland? These are fair questions, which a 2022 study published in *Frontiers in Sustainable Food Systems* sought to answer.

Within the Greenbelt itself, the study found that farmland is very well protected. After an initial flurry of development that had been grandfathered in, the rate of farmland loss within the Greenbelt dropped to only about 1 hectare per year. Outside of the Greenbelt, things get more complicated, but loss of farmland also declined. The success of farmland conservation outside the Greenbelt owes a lot to policies introduced in conjunction with the Greenbelt Plan.

The *Places to Grow Act*, passed in 2005, led to regional growth plans that include increased urban density as an alternative to urban

Only half a percent of Canada's land is class one farmland.

sprawl—called the "other side of the coin to farmland protection in urban planning." Outside of growth plan areas and the Greenbelt, the 2005 (and subsequent) Provincial Policy Statements also emphasized intensification within settlement areas as a means to reduce sprawl and the conversion of farmland. The result of these three combined policies was that loss of farmland outside of the Greenbelt dropped by almost half from 2005 to 2017. Whether that can continue into the future is less certain.

The future of Ontario's Greenbelt

THE CHALLENGE OF GROWTH

Between 1996 and 2021, the population of the Greater Golden Horseshoe (roughly the area surrounded by the Greenbelt) grew by 57%. The Ontario government is predicting another 45% increase (to almost 15 million residents) by 2051. With the federal government's goal of significantly increasing Canada's population, and a tendency for people to aggregate in a handful of urban areas in the country, we shouldn't be surprised by ongoing land use conflict between urban sprawl, agriculture, and greenspace in southern Ontario. For the first 17 years of its existence, the Greenbelt and other land use policies enacted alongside it worked surprisingly well to limit the negative impacts of sprawl. And in 2022–23, the Greenbelt withstood its first serious challenge with the reversal of controversial land withdrawals (euphemistically dubbed the "land swap"). But what can we expect in the future? Some of the world's oldest greenbelts, found in Britain, may offer some clues.

In his book *Outskirts*, author John Grindrod unravels the history of greenbelts in Britain, intermingled with his own story of growing up on the edge of the London Greenbelt. It's a messy book—as it winds its way through his life and the complicated policy questions of the greenbelts in Britain, I was often unsure of where it was going. By the end, I began to think this could be intentional, that the entire book was a sort of allegory for greenbelts. After digging through the fraught history of greenbelts and choices that would one day have to be made about them, his ultimate conclusion was: the greenbelt is "undoubtedly better than nothing."

The British greenbelts have withstood the test of decades, which bodes well for the future of Ontario's greenbelt, though the pressures on them are growing, and those intervening decades have not always been kind. Building housing on greenbelts is always hard—because that's the point! But for some reason, it's often okay to build highways willy nilly, as if one of the functions of a greenbelt is to maintain a road allowance. It was true in Britain, and Ontario seems to be following suit with the proposed Highway 413. But are highways necessarily better than houses?

The UK organization Centre for Cities proposed limited public-transit-oriented development within British greenbelts, subject to intensive local public participation and rigorous environmental zoning. It seems like a reasonable proposal, but is this kind of slow chipping away anathema to greenbelts? Arguably, yes, but I can't help thinking that waiting for a crisis may result in far worse decisions being made.

The Alliance for a Liveable Ontario takes a different approach, proposing a switch away from building low-density unaffordable housing that sprawls over farmland toward building homes people can afford closer to urban centers. "Every big house that gets built out in the suburbs diverts labour and construction material from building the types of housing we need" says David Crombie, a founder of the Alliance and former mayor of Toronto.

Ontario's Greenbelt incorporated some of Britain's hard-learned lessons at the outset. It is better planned and envisioned, with the aid of hindsight from other jurisdictions, a vast planning bureaucracy that didn't exist in

Development along the east bank of Pickering's Duffins Creek will impact the water quality of one of the cleanest creeks in the GTA.

post-war Britain, and a plan to accommodate growth for decades to come. There is still a lot of land available to be developed eventually, the so-called "white belt" around the GTA. As it turned out, the first challenge to the Greenbelt came decades before the white belt was used up, but it passed the test, and the failed land withdrawals of 2022 may have strengthened the Greenbelt. Greenbelts remain popular in both Britain and Ontario for lack of any other alternative to uncontrolled sprawl—but Grindrod warns us that "Once we had them in place, then the real struggles would begin."

OLD-GROWTH FORESTS IN ONTARIO

When lumbermen in the 1800s were cutting huge pine trees in Ontario, they knew it had taken them centuries to grow. Gradually that awareness faded over time, but never quite went away. Many small local battles were waged to protect forests in the 20th century, mostly for their recreational and scenic value rather than their antiquity or biodiversity value. Take Temagami, Ontario, for example—the shorelines of Lake Temagami were preserved because cottagers wanted to keep their view, and nearby White Bear Forest was left alone because it was across from the lumber mill, and the owner of the mill liked the "nice pine across the lake." By contrast, in north-western Ontario the Greenwood Lake forest was preserved in the 1970s because local resource managers recognized the old pines were a rare remnant of virgin forest. That was a very unusual case—in many parts of Ontario, loggers were still cutting the remnants as fast as they could, which was rather fast indeed. The business of logging had rapidly mechanized from the 1960s to the 1980s, with more trees being cut by fewer and fewer people. By the 1980s, a public backlash was growing.

The term "old-growth forest" was (as far as I can tell) coined in the 1940s in the United States, but it didn't reach the public consciousness until the 1980s. In the intervening four decades, the term was rarely used, and usually by foresters for whom it was synonymous with terms like "decadent" and "overmature"—something that got in the way of productive forestry. This began to change in 1981 when researchers at the Pacific Northwest Research Station in Oregon published "Ecological characteristics of old-growth Douglas-fir forests," an influential paper that began laying the foundation for old-growth forest conservation. The term was picked up by conservationists in the Pacific Northwest United States and in British Columbia.

Within the decade, it would be applied to the centuries-old pine forests remaining in Temagami, Ontario—by 1989, a protest against logging these forests would set Canadian records for duration and number of arrests up to that time. Apparently by chance, around the same time, the ancient cedars were discovered on the Niagara Escarpment. These small bonsai-like trees had been clinging to the cliff face largely unnoticed, which is remarkable when you consider that trees approaching one thousand years-old were

Old-growth oak savannah can be found at Lambton Park in Toronto's west end.

growing in Milton, within sight of one of Canada's busiest highways. In this book, we'll visit ancient cedars at Rattlesnake Point, the Horse Lake Trail, and at the tip of the Greenbelt on Flowerpot Island.

Over the past few decades, various types of old-growth forest have been recognized in Ontario, many of which are featured in this book. Widely spaced oaks growing in grassland make up oak savannah, which is best seen at Paradise Grove and Lambton Park. Carolinian forest, with its characteristic tulip trees and sassafras, can be found at McMaster Forest. Deep shady hemlock forest is found at Twenty Valley, Bronte Creek, in parts of Short Hills Park, and

Beaver Valley. Some of the oldest forest (other than ancient cedars) is at the easternmost extent of the Oak Ridges Moraine, where Peter's Woods has oak and maple trees that have lived for over 400 years. Some of the urban forests that can be reached by Toronto's subway system were logged at settlement but left alone since, and have trees that are 180-to 200-years-old. With such a wide variety of forests featured in this book, it's fair to wonder: what exactly does it mean when we use the term old-growth forest?

WHAT IS AN OLD-GROWTH FOREST?

I published my first book about old-growth forests in 2010, and since that time, I've had many opportunities to answer the same question phrased in various ways: what is an old-growth forest; how do you define it; how old is it? You'd think by now I'd have perfected the elevator pitch. I haven't, but I'm less likely to see people's eyes glaze over as I struggle to give a simple answer to a complex question. There are a lot of ways of defining old-growth forest because the landscape isn't homogenous. Why would we expect a definition that fits Niagara Falls to work in Algonquin Park? Everything, from the forest type to settlement history, is different, but there is certainly old-growth forest in both places.

There are many different definitions for old-growth forest but, basically, they can be shoe-horned into two broad categories: those that describe very old, undisturbed forest where trees may be dying of old age; and those that describe middle-aged forest (typically over 150 years) that may or may not have had some human disturbance. Neither type of definition is better than the other.

Definitions that require a pristine forest devoid of human disturbance would exclude just about everything we consider old-growth forest in Ontario south of Algonquin Park, except perhaps cliff-growing ancient cedars. Most forests have at least had a little firewood cutting or selective tree removal during the long history of settlement. Forests in southern Ontario, however,

Pileated woodpecker is one of the species that thrives in old-growth forests.

are known to have trees over 500-years-old—to say there's no old growth there would clearly be false.

On the other hand, definitions that emphasize a late stage of stand development (trees dying of old age and being replaced by new trees), would exclude majestic 250-year-old red and white pine stands in Temagami—pines can live for at least 500 years, so those are middle-aged stands.

The solution to the apparent contradiction is that old-growth forest is not an end point, but a continuum. On our managed forest landscape, forests that have passed the optimum age for commercial harvesting are relatively rare—so it makes sense to begin definitions at or beyond this threshold. It's no coincidence that tree growth begins to slow around this age (which is variable by species), so when trees are occasionally felled by wind, insects, disease, etc., gaps will remain in the canopy for a while. The number of large logs and snags (dead standing trees) will increase over time, often for centuries.

Eventually, in theory, the forest will enter a steady state where trees are continuously dying and growing, and it is a very uneven-aged forest. This is the ultimate old-growth forest implied in some definitions.

Though tree species may transition as a forest continues to age, and average tree age will level out, many other old-growth characteristics will continue to increase. The characteristics of old-growth forest may include:

- old trees
- large diameter dead trees, both fallen (logs) and standing (snags)
- openings in the forest canopy
- undisturbed soil layers
- uneven forest floor, characterized by pits and mounds left by windthrown trees
- multiple vegetation layers, from understory and shrub to canopy and supercanopy
- high diversity in the herbaceous layer

Old-growth forests have standing and fallen dead trees in varying stages of decay, and often have trees of various sizes and ages.

- lichen and fungus abundance and diversity
- late-successional (shade tolerant) tree species, and
- absence of human disturbance.

Most of these characteristics are only just getting started when an old-growth forest reaches a minimum age, and will continue to increase usually for centuries. Arguably, all definitions of old-growth forest are correct, they just aren't defining the same stage of old growth.

How to make sense of all this? Look around in your own local area and ask, what is the most intact forest where natural processes still operate, often despite human interference, and where trees are allowed to grow old? If you're in Toronto, maybe it's High Park, and if you're in Temagami, it's probably the Obabika forest. On some level, this is how most old-growth forest definitions came to be—they were reverse-engineered to match the scattered, often damaged remnants of the forests that were once common on the landscape.

I think that's fine, at least until we let more of the landscape grow truly old—maybe, with some planning and some luck, our great-great grandchildren will find they want to tighten up the definitions.

OLD-GROWTH FORESTS AND ONTARIO'S GREENBELT

The Greenbelt protects old-growth forests from myriad impacts caused by fragmentation and urbanization, meanwhile, old-growth forests also enhance the value of the Greenbelt in important ways. Old-growth forests function as core natural areas, protecting high levels of biodiversity and preserving genetic diversity—research has shown that old-growth trees have higher genetic diversity, so are more likely to be able to adapt to a changing climate, introduced diseases, etc.

Access to greenspace has significant benefits for human health, including reduced mortality, increased physical activity, and greater happiness. There is evidence that high quality natural areas, such as old-growth forests, may have

The shoreline of Duffins Creek along the Seaton Trail is part of nature's playground.

more positive effects than less biodiverse areas (this rings true to me based on my own experiences). Forests create cool islands in urban environments, reducing local air temperatures by as much as 12 degrees Celsius.

Old-growth forests help mitigate climate change by absorbing and sequestering carbon at higher rates than younger forests. Old-growth forests contribute to the role of Ontario's Greenbelt as a carbon sink.

HOW TO WALK IN THE WOODS

Above all, enjoy the forest! Here are some tips that may help you do that.

- Bring enough water and snacks
- Take your time. Stop often/long enough to appreciate the forest
- Try going out before dawn in May and June, for a symphony of bird song
- Stay off your phone unless it's needed for route finding, photography, or species identification
- If you bring a smartphone, download the iNaturalist and Merlin apps
- Look up, look down, look at details

Old-growth forests are special and rare places, and a little extra care is needed when we visit them. Here are basic guidelines for walking in any forest, but especially the forests listed in this book.

- Stay on the trail!
- Keep dogs on a leash (or leave them home)
- Don't collect anything
- Don't disturb logs

There are a couple of exceptions to these rules. It may be okay to leave the trail in the dead of winter (on snowshoes, for example), if you're careful not to break shrubs and saplings. This can allow you to explore and gain a deeper understanding of the forest, and learn animal tracks, winter tree identification, etc. Conversely, in spring, the young growth of plants and nests of birds are especially vulnerable so you should never leave the trail or let your dog run free in any forest during May and June. Don't collect anything is an important rule, but you may wonder, is it really wrong to collect a few seeds to grow at home? In Provincial and National Parks, collecting anything is illegal but, with great care, it may be possible in some other parks. Make sure you know what you're collecting from; only collect from plants that are abundant; only collect a very small proportion of the seeds; and never collect from species at risk.

OTHER TIPS ON USING THIS BOOK

When ages are given for a forest, it is usually an accurate age based on tree ring counts. Sometimes I, or another researcher, was able to extract a tree core (a pencil-shaped piece of wood that is drilled from the tree) and count the annual growth rings. In many other cases, rings were counted from the cross-section of a tree that fell across the trail and was cut as part of trail maintenance. You, too, can do this! The rings of conifers are particularly easy to count, as well as oak and ash. Maples and birches can be tricky to count without sanding the wood.

Bike Share is suggested as an option for exploring some of the Toronto sites; learn more at bikesharetoronto.com and download the app to check bike availability at each location ahead of time.

Coordinates for sites are given in case you have trouble pinpointing trailheads, parking, etc. If you type these into any map search engine (Google Maps, Bing Maps, etc.) as written, they will show you a dropped pin and allow you to get directions or navigate to that point.

Contours on most of the maps show 5-metre elevation change. However, due to the data that was publicly available, maps within Toronto (the Don and Humber valleys) show 1-metre elevation change.

Updates, references, and news related to this book can be found at oldgrowth.ca/greenbelt.

The annual growth rings on this hemlock log reveal the age of the tree when it died: over 250 years!

Niagara Peninsula

Paradise Grove

✤ What you'll like

Paradise Grove is an impressive old-growth oak savannah where white, red, and bur oak trees reach over 275-years-old and a metre wide, just a short walk from Niagara-on-the-Lake. Oak savannah restoration is in progress here, meaning parts of the forest are excellent examples of oak savannah forest, while the rest is dense with invasive Norway maple—but the oaks are still very impressive! A string of charismatic heritage oaks ranging in age from 200 to over 320-years-old begins at the Grove and stretches along the Niagara River Recreation Trail, making for a pleasant walk or bike ride with views over the Niagara River.

✤ How to get there

By car – Parking is available off John Street (43.2439, -79.0679), or Ricardo Street (43.2420, -79.0601), in Niagara-on-the-Lake near the Niagara Parkway.

By public transit – St Catharines can be reached by GO train/bus in a little over two hours from Toronto. At Niagara College Glendale Campus

Old-growth oak trees along the Niagara River Recreation Trail can be over 300-years-old.

GO stop, you can transfer to Niagara-on-the-Lake Transit and continue to old town Niagara-on-the-Lake. Use the Community Transport Group/ Niagara-on-the-Lake Transit web page to check for your connection: https://ctgcanada.ca/about/transit/. It's a pleasant walk or bike ride to Paradise Grove from Niagara-on-the-Lake.

By bike — Paradise Grove is located near the beginning of the Niagara River Recreation Trail, a 56 km multi-use trail that parallels the Niagara Parkway. It is a short bike ride from Niagara-on-the-Lake, or a little over an hour from Niagara Falls.

✤ What to do

Consider visiting in the off-season or on a weekday so you can enjoy the restaurants and pubs in Niagara-on-the-Lake. The oak forest is particularly beautiful on warm autumn days after Canadian Thanksgiving. A couple of hours should give you time to visit the limited trail system, including a few secondary trails you may wish to explore. You may want to walk or bike some of the recreation trail, which will let you enjoy the heritage oaks preserved along its length from Paradise Grove to Queenston. Make a stop at McFarland House, where you can enjoy a guided tour, order afternoon tea, and see some old growth oaks on the site. This forest couples well with Brock's Monument, which is also a relatively short hike.

✤ Learn more

Fort George was first built in 1796, as part of the British defences against American attacks across the Niagara River. At the time, there was a young oak savannah just south of the fort, where white, black, red, and bur oak trees were around 60-years-old, and native grasses such as big bluestem, little bluestem, and Indian grass swayed in the dappled sun beneath the trees. There was a small black gum swamp nestled in among the oaks.

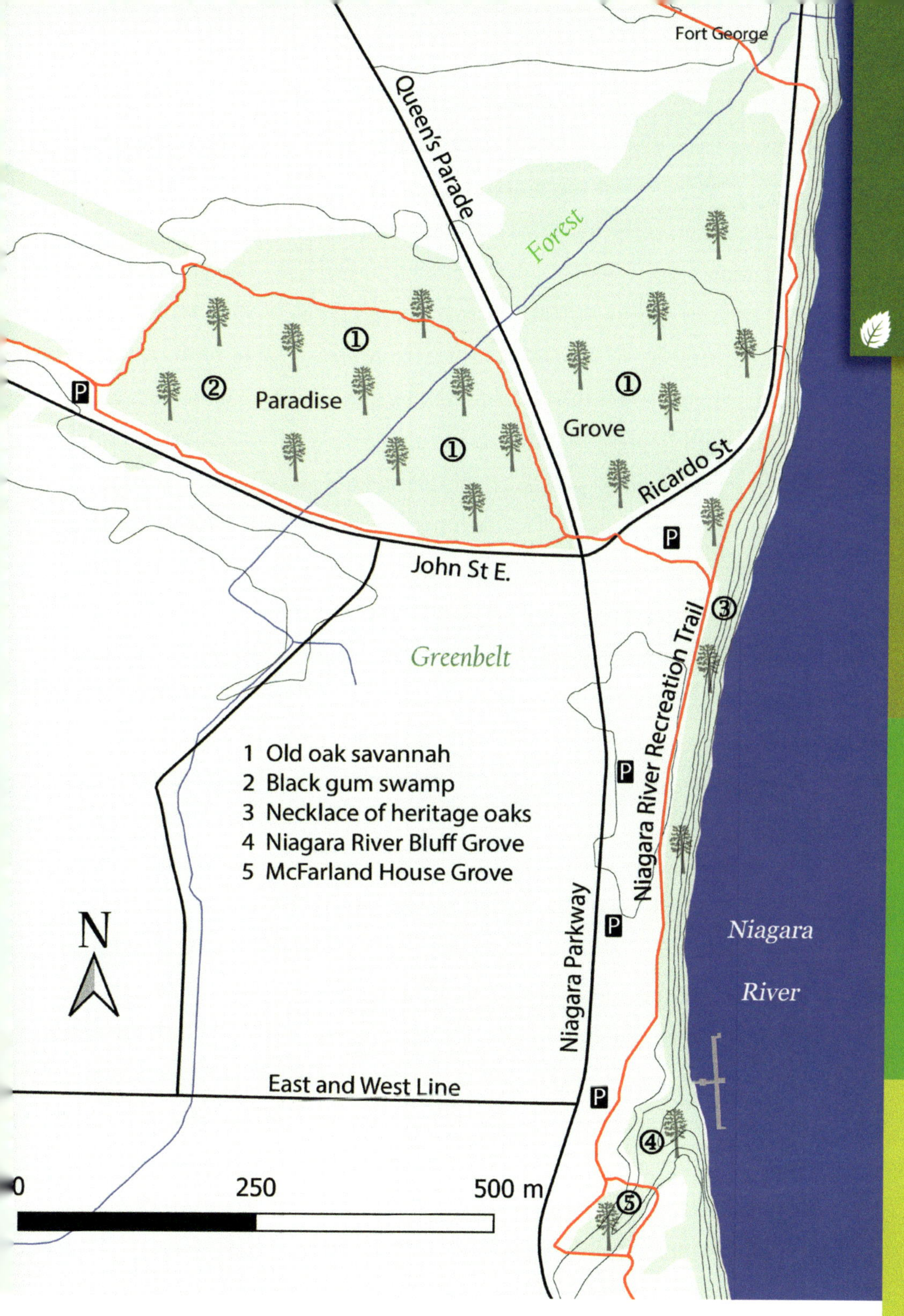
Fort George
Queen's Parade
Forest
Paradise
Grove
Ricardo St
John St E.
Greenbelt
Niagara River Recreation Trail
1 Old oak savannah
2 Black gum swamp
3 Necklace of heritage oaks
4 Niagara River Bluff Grove
5 McFarland House Grove
N
Niagara Parkway
East and West Line
Niagara River
0
250
500 m

Today we call this forest Paradise Grove, and you can walk among many of the same trees that stood there in the war of 1812, when Fort George was captured and most of the buildings were destroyed. You can also visit a reconstruction of the historic Fort George.

Paradise Grove itself is due for some restoration. The grassland that once grew in the understory of the oak savannah is now all but gone, replaced with dense shrubs and invasive Norway maple trees. A plan is taking form to cut out the invasive species that are choking the understory and hopefully implement a regimen of occasional controlled burns to bring back the native grass species. It's surprising how many native grasses are still in these forests, banked as seeds in the soil, waiting for the opportunity to sprout after a fire. In the past, when the Niagara Parks Commission stopped mowing some of the parkland under scattered oak trees, many of the native grasses returned. Because of this, some of the sparse oak forest around the parking lot and in a wedge along the Niagara River Recreation Trail is one of the more ecologically intact parts of Paradise Grove. Hopefully more of the grove will be restored to its original oak savannah over time.

Despite the problems, there are few places in Ontario with a more impressive oak forest. The diversity of old-growth oak species, exceptional tree sizes (over a metre in diameter), and ages (up to 300-years-old), is unique. Hopefully prescribed burns and removal of Norway maple will help kick-start a new generation of oaks in this forest. Paradise Grove already has two main generations of old-growth trees, with the oldest trees dating back to the mid-1700s, and another generation that germinated in the 1800s, possibly after selective logging and/or grazing. Oak forests thrive on a certain amount of disturbance, and clearing out invasive species could provide the impetus these trees need to start the next generation.

A chain of sparsely scattered old-growth oak trees is also found along

The Paradise Savannah Black Oak is over 230-years-old and is easily recognized by its massive burl.

the recreation trail, remnants of the same forest that is still found in Paradise Grove. The late Bruce Kershner, an old-growth forest expert from New York State, identified 138 old oak trees between Paradise Grove and Queenston that he called a necklace of heritage oaks, strung along the bike path. Cores taken from the trees showed that they range in age from 200 to 340-years-old (most commonly 240-to 270-years-old). These trees are within six metres or less of the Niagara River Recreation Trail, so they can easily be seen and visited. Historically, their shade was probably enjoyed by travellers walking the road from Niagara-on-the-Lake to Queenston.

Today, tourists enjoy the shade along the Niagara Recreation Trail, largely unaware of the exceptional age of these charismatic oaks.

One of the most obvious oaks is found beside the Recreation Trail between the Ricardo Street parking lot and the Niagara River, which Kershner named the Paradise Savannah Black Oak. It's 1.7 metres in diameter and 230-years-old; you can recognize it by a massive burl at ground level on one side, and a huge branch jutting out horizontally. This and other large oaks in this meadow grove were once part of a larger oak savannah community connected to Paradise Grove.

There are also small groves of old-growth oaks near McFarland House, and in a ravine to the northeast of the historic home. One of the best pockets of old growth in the ravine is adjacent to an off-limits maintenance area, but you can get a view of it from the pedestrian/cycling bridge that crosses the ravine. All of this is only a short bike ride or walk from Paradise Grove.

Brock's Monument Old-growth Oak Forest

✣ What you'll like

Brock's Monument marks the southern terminus of the Bruce Trail, the starting point for many epic journeys. It is also an old-growth forest where you can walk among 250-year-old oaks that were witness trees to the Battle of Queenston Heights. It's a good place to see a wide variety of trees, including white, red, and black oak, butternut, and slippery elm.

✣ How to get there

By car – Parking is available at Queenston Heights Park (follow signs for Brock's Monument). Park at the west end of the parking lots off Portage Road (43.158, -79.058).

By public transit – Public Transit from Niagara Falls will get you close, and Niagara bus tours also stop here, though in the latter case, you may not have time to explore the forest.

By bike – It can be reached by bike in under an hour from Niagara Falls or Niagara-on-the-Lake; the most pleasant route is along the Niagara River Recreation Trail.

✣ What to do

This forest is charming on a quiet autumn day, but less restful in peak summer rush; consider a trip to Niagara in the off-season. A visit to this forest could be combined with a bike ride along the Niagara Parkway, and/or a visit to Paradise Grove. Along the way is a chain of remnant 200- to 350-year-old oak trees that can be seen from the bike trail (see the Paradise Grove description). In the off-season, you should visit one of the pubs or restaurants in Niagara-on-the-Lake. In peak tourist season, you might

The author with a white oak that witnessed the Battle of Queenston Heights in 1812

want to pack a picnic lunch to eat at Queenston Heights Park or anywhere along the Parkway Trail.

✣ Learn more

"Day was just glimmering. The cannon from both sides of the river roared incessantly. Queenston was illuminated by the continual discharge of small arms."

—John Beverly Robinson, 1812

"Witness tree" is the name given to a tree that stood during a great historic battle. Most commonly it's used for trees that survived the American Civil War, but in Brock's Monument Forest, I found myself leaning against a big white oak that is a witness tree. In fact, it did more than witness the Battle of Queenston Heights, it participated in it! This tree would have been about 40- to 50-years-old in 1812, when 80 Mohawk and allied warriors led by Chief John Norton used the oak grove here as cover to fire on American militia forces for three and a half hours. Are there musket balls still embedded deep within this tree? I'll probably never know—but old trees, like old buildings, are surrounded by stories.

The battle of Queenston Heights was a hot mess ("spectacularly unsuccessful or disordered, and a source of peculiar fascination"), and both sides would pay a high cost before the day was done. Hours before dawn on the morning of October 13, 1812, boatloads of American soldiers crossed the churning Niagara River under small-arms fire. Despite losing their leader to a musket ball in the first crossing, they took the hill by filing along the shore and up a fishermen's trail to Queenston Heights, where they surprised a small artillery crew and captured the valuable high ground.

Sometime before 7 AM, in the grey gloom before dawn, General Brock arrived on horseback and assumed command of the British force. He was a charismatic and clever leader. Earlier that year, Brock had convinced a much

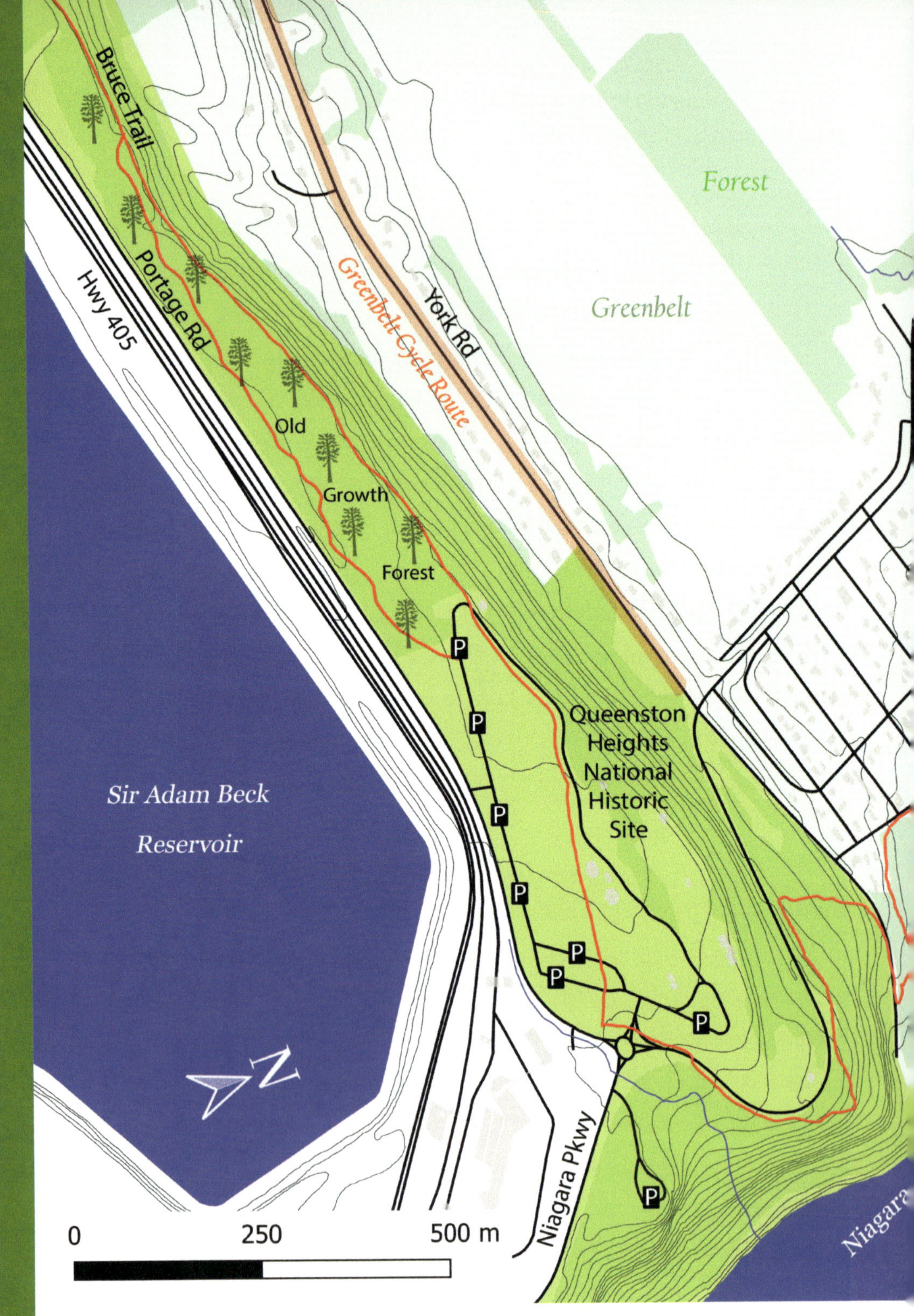
Bruce Trail
Portage Rd
Hwy 405
Greenbelt Cycle Route
York Rd
Forest
Greenbelt
Old
Growth
Forest
Queenston
Heights
National
Historic
Site
Sir Adam Beck
Reservoir
N
Niagara Pkwy
Niagara
0
250
500 m

larger and better armed force to surrender Detroit by marching his troops in the daytime, then sneaking them back at night to march in again the next day, fooling the American general into vastly overestimating his forces.

But on October 13, his bravery outshone his wisdom, or his luck ran out, or maybe a showy sash he'd been given by Tecumseh helped draw American musket fire to him. In any case, around dawn, General Brock led a charge up the hill to retake Queenston Heights and was shot. He continued to charge, wounded, and was shot again, this time fatally.

Around 11 AM, John Norton and the Mohawk of the Grand River attacked the Americans from the oak forest to the west. A series of charges from the front, attacks from the flank, and ongoing harassment for over three hours broke the morale of the American militia and helped turn the battle back in favour of the British. I can imagine Norton taking aim from behind a relatively young oak tree and firing. Splinters fly from the trees around him as an American force ten times as large returns fire. Over the next few hours, he and his men would move within the forest, making it seem like a larger force was attacking.

Today you can walk among some of the same trees they were using for cover, scattered large oaks that are now growing mixed with a younger forest of sugar maples. Musket balls in the old oaks here is not such a stretch; they were commonly found in trees at the Civil War battlefield in Gettysburg, Pennsylvania. Most recently, a musket ball was found in a fallen oak tree there in 2011, 150 years after the battle was fought. The maintenance crew happened to hit it with their chainsaw as they cleared the tree.

Trees like that have been named witness trees, and it's a good name; the trees at Queenston Heights have witnessed a lot since they started growing in the mid 1700s, not least the battle that is memorialized by the 56-metre-high Brock's monument. Later, when the oaks were approaching 200-years-old, the Bruce Trail was founded, and its southern terminus is marked by a cairn not far from this forest. Since 1967, over 4000 people have hiked the entire

900 km trail from end to end (though not always in one go), and either the beginning or the end of their hike has been quietly witnessed by the old oaks.

You enter the forest past a sign marking the entrance to the Bruce Trail and are immediately greeted by a large white oak to the right of the trail. During my visit, I saw that a major branch had fallen from high in the tree and was cut into lengths by the maintenance crew. I stopped to count the growth rings on one of the pieces and found the branch had grown for at least 154 years, longer than most trees in southern Ontario!

This forest was once an oak savannah, but now has younger sugar maple, red maple, beech, walnut, butternut, and slippery elm growing among the older oaks. Though they are younger, these other species, especially the maples, still reach up to 180-years-old! Two butternuts in the forest appear to be very old, but both are off trail. The forest is dominated by red, white, and some black oak (the latter especially around the informal trail to the south). There's a big question mark about whether scarlet oak is also found here, but if so, it may be the only place in Ontario where this species is found!

A couple of smaller informal trails can be picked up pretty easily at the back end of the old forest and used to form a loop closer to Portage Road, finishing behind the picnic area south of the parking lot. Along these informal trails, there are a number of freshly windthrown trees. As the wind tipped the trees, the roots pulled up a lot of soil, creating a large pit and a mound where the soil is piled up around the root mass. This "pit and mound topography" is common in many old-growth forests, and can persist for hundreds of years, even after the tree itself has rotted away. It's a fascinating clue to the history of the forest, and if the pits fill with water in spring, they create ephemeral pools where salamanders and other amphibians can lay their eggs.

An old-growth red oak tree in Brock's Monument forest

Short Hills Provincial Park (12 Mile Creek Headwaters)

✣ What you'll like

Short Hills Park has seemingly endless hiking trails through a diverse rolling landscape, across pastoral open fields and old orchards occasionally dissected by deep-cut shady valleys. In these valleys, clear, cold streams are inhabited by brook trout and Louisiana waterthrush. Small pockets of old-growth forest on the valley bottoms and slopes can reach 300-years-old, framing picturesque waterfalls. In nearby St. Johns Conservation Area impressive tulip trees and other hardwoods can be seen along the Tulip Tree Trail.

✣ How to get there

By car – Short Hills is less than an hour from Hamilton via the QEW. Use exit 51/Regional Road 34, go south, turn left on Regional Road 81, then right on First Street to reach the east side of the Park. For Terrace Creek, follow Cataract Road and Wiley Road to Short Hills Parking Lot C (43.1022, -79.2721). The Swayze Falls entrance is at Short Hills Parking Lot B (43.0903, -79.3051). Parking for St. Johns Conservation Area is at the end of Baron Road (43.0667, -79.2849)

By public transit – The north end of Short Hills Park and Decew Falls is only a half-hour walk from Brock University, which is serviced by St Catharines Transit and GO Bus. The old-growth forest at Terrace Creek can be reached in one to two hours walk from the University.

By bike – It is a short (uphill) bike ride to Short Hills from St Catharines (GO Buses from Toronto can carry up to two bikes on a front rack). The Park is located between several cycle routes promoted by the Niagara Cycling

Terrace Creek Falls is surrounded by old-growth forest.

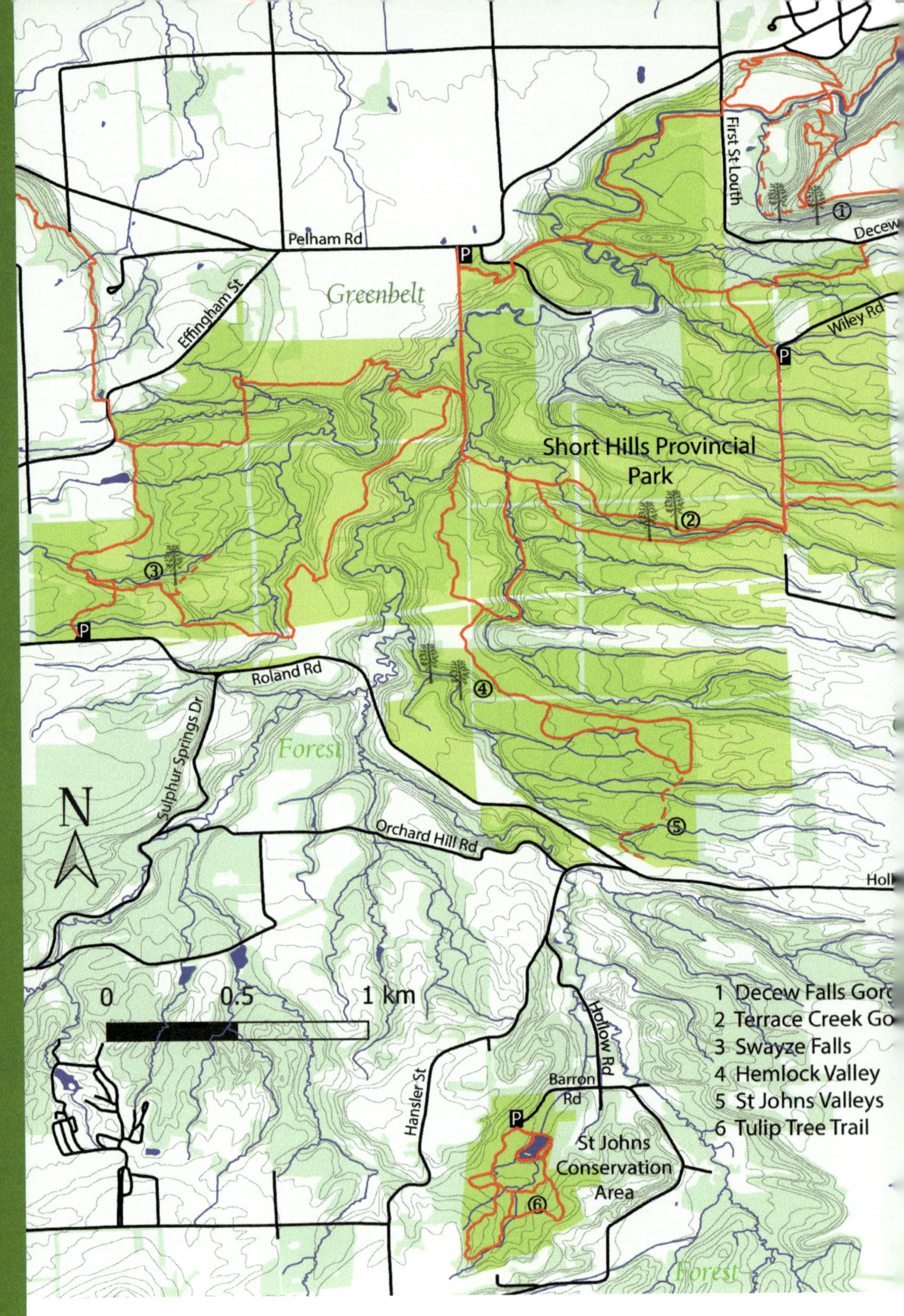
Pelham Rd
Greenbelt
Effingham St
First St Louth
Decew
Wiley Rd
Short Hills Provincial Park
Roland Rd
Forest
Sulphur Springs Dr
Orchard Hill Rd
Holl
N
0
0.5
1 km
Hollow Rd
Barron Rd
Hansler St
St Johns Conservation Area
Forest
1 Decew Falls Gorg
2 Terrace Creek Go
3 Swayze Falls
4 Hemlock Valley
5 St Johns Valleys
6 Tulip Tree Trail

Tourism Centre: the Pelham Route, the Wine Route, and the Greater Niagara Circle Route (including the Welland Canal Bike Path).

✤ What to do

From the end of Wiley Rd, hike the Terrace Creek Trail (via Black Walnut Trail) and enjoy the old-growth forest around Terrace Creek Falls. From there you may wish to continue on to Hemlock Valley, or you could hop back in your car and visit St. Johns Conservation Area, Swayze Falls, or Decew Falls, all of which have old-growth forest. The old growth at Swayze and Decew is in the ravine bottom and access is via informal, sometimes treacherous trails. Visiting a winery is always an option as there are several nearby.

✤ Learn more

The Louisiana waterthrush is a small warbler that lives along cold, fast-moving streams in steep ravines, under a canopy of mature forest. It searches for food by walking along the banks of streams or in the shallow water, hunting for insects, spiders, seeds, small molluscs, fish, crustaceans, and sometimes small amphibians. "This diet is somewhat unique for a North American songbird," ornithologist Edward Cheskey wrote in 2003, in a report about the 12 Mile Creek Headwaters (which includes Short Hills Provincial Park and St. Johns Conservation Area).

Seen from a satellite, the valleys of 12 Mile Creek Headwaters look like a can of green paint spilled and flowed across the landscape. The streaks of green are steep-sided valleys that provide habitat for the Louisiana waterthrush and other rare and endangered birds such as hooded warblers, Acadian flycatchers, and rusty blackbirds. Twelve Mile Creek is also the only cold-water brook trout stream on the Niagara Peninsula, and one of a few places in Ontario where American eels have been found in recent decades.

This isn't the impression of Short Hills Park that greets you in the parking lot. You can walk for quite a while on the undulating landscape and see only old farms, pasture, and abandoned orchards. The deep-cut ravines sneak up on you. In the early 2000s the whole area was recognized both as an Important Birding Area by Birdlife International, and as an "old-growth forest reserve" by Bruce Kershner.

Before his untimely death in 2007, Kershner was an old-growth sleuth with few rivals, based in western New York State. He aged trees with a mix of tree coring, counting the rings of fallen logs, and estimating age based on visual characteristics, at which he was remarkably good. Of the three methods, Kershner tried to use tree-coring the least. More often he could be found gazing at trees or bent over, counting rings on a fallen log cut by a maintenance crew. These same techniques are available to the rest of us!

Short Hills Park itself has five distinct, albeit small, old-growth forests, and several others are near or adjacent to the Park, including Decew Falls gorge, Rockway Conservation Area, and St. Johns Conservation Area. One of the finest and most easily visited is the Terrace Creek Gorge.

The southwest branch of the Terrace Creek Trail (also a leg of the Bruce Trail) follows the creek, and once you enter the woods, you'll start to see old sugar maple and hemlock trees on the valley slopes and bottom. Kershner estimated the ages at around 300 years. He also estimated red and black oak in this forest (on the upper slopes) to reach over 200-years-old, and a 20-cm-diameter flowering dogwood was 175-years-old. The best views of old forest are looking into the steep valley between the power lines and the waterfall, as well as below the falls, where some sugar maples on the opposite slope and terrace exhibit old-age characteristics like bark balding and a sinuous trunk. In the spring, a variety of spring ephemerals, including Dutchman's breeches, bloodroot, and hepatica showcase their wares for the pollinators.

After Terrace Creek you may want to go on to Hemlock Valley. The trail winds through old fields and abandoned orchards, then skirts the edge of a deep, shady hemlock valley. It follows the forest edge for a while, offering limited views into old-growth forest, and then curves away in a large loop, leaving you wanting more. There is no access into the valley, and it should be left alone, a relatively pristine fragile ecosystem—unless, maybe in the dead of winter, you want to make a careful excursion on snowshoes.

The mix of fields and deep wooded valleys has a timeless feel, and I wonder if this landscape would feel familiar to loyalist settlers in the late 1700s. My mind strays to the Upper Canada rebellion of 1837–38, and how it unfolded on the edge of Short Hills. In June 1838, a large group of rebels captured four Queen's Lancers staying at Osterhout's Tavern (just south of Hemlock Valley on Holland Rd), an event that was later named the Short Hills raid. In the end, there was no bloodshed, though one of the rebels was later hanged (one of many executions of the rebellion's leaders). Another was exiled to Tasmania, though he escaped and fled to Iowa. As far as I know, the tavern is gone without a trace.

The 1837 rebellion actually began in Lower Canada (now Quebec) and was joined almost simultaneously in Upper Canada (Ontario), with many of the same grievances. The Québécois still feel the sting of it, and the execution of the leaders is part of the separatist cause commemorated by the Journée Nationale des Patriotes. In Ontario it was commemorated by Upper Canada Brewery's Rebellion Ale, which Ontarians drank liberally in the 1990s with no sense of grievance as far as I know. I wonder if this was understood in part as a class struggle common to Anglophone and Francophone Canadians at the time, if that might help in a small way to bridge the modern divide between Quebec and the rest of Canada. Who knows?

Meanwhile, the new battle of Short Hills is between deer and understory plants. In the absence of predators, deer populations in the Park had grown to the point where the deer devoured all the delicious native plants, leaving

Old-growth forest in Terrace Creek valley

little behind except in some cases the unpalatable invasives. This has become a problem in many of Southern Ontario's forests, but since 2013, Ontario has recognized the rights of the Haudenosaunee Confederacy (Six Nations) to bow-hunt white-tailed deer in Short Hills Park.

Not everyone is happy about this, but the hunt, and associated protests against it, have become an annual event each fall. The park is probably much better for it, and the venison is shared among the five longhouses at the Six Nations reserve during midwinter ceremonies. But you may want to check before planning a hike from October through mid-December, as the Park may be closed on certain days for the hunt.

The Tulip Tree Trail, in nearby St. Johns Conservation Area, is another place to see old-growth forest. Though the trees are younger than Terrace Creek this is in some ways a more impressive forest. Tulip trees, red oaks and sugar maples all reach around 200-years-old (or more) and impressive sizes, some up to a metre in diameter. The trails are relatively short, and mostly through younger forest, but if you're in the area anyway, it would be a shame not to visit this Conservation Area.

Balls Falls Conservation Area (Twenty Valley)

✤ What you'll like

At Balls Falls you'll hike through old-growth forest over 300-years-old in a dramatic steep valley littered with limestone boulders. Nearby historic buildings, museums, restaurants, and wineries offer ample opportunities to spoil yourself after a vigorous hike. This is a fairly challenging hike with steep climbs and uneven ground. In very low water (common through mid summer), exploring the bouldery creek bed is a popular pastime, though in high water, the same boulders create terrifying white water. If the creek is more than a trickle, stay away from the waters edge!

✤ How to get there

By car – You can get there in about an hour by car from closer parts of Toronto. Take exit 57 from the QEW. Park either at Balls Falls Conservation Area (paid parking, but close to the old-growth forest and historic buildings, 43.1335, -79.3860), Bruce Trail access off Glen Road (limited parking, 43.1391, -79.3740), or Jordan Hollow Park off King Street (43.1423, -79.3725).

By public transit – There is no direct public transit connection. The closest stops are in Beamsville or St Catharines, and from there you could use a taxi or bike to get to Twenty Valley.

By bike – The Greenbelt Cycle Route runs along King Street; you could park your bike at Jordan Hollow Park and hike the trail upstream to the old-growth forest. The shoulder along King Street tends to be narrow.

✤ What to do

The hike is short but a worthy destination on its own. However, if you

The steep climb in and out of Twenty Valley helped protect the old-growth forest.

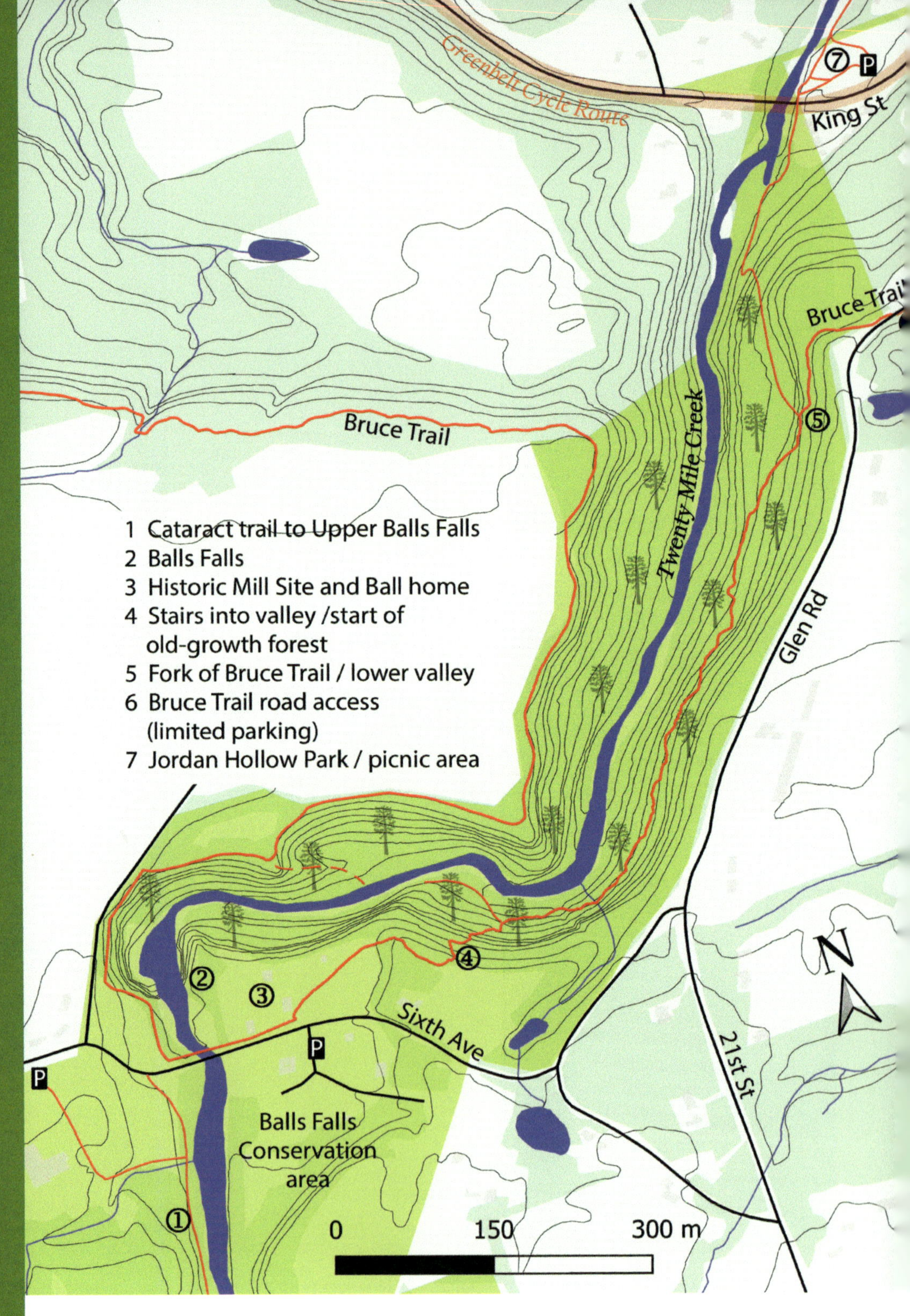
Greenbelt Cycle Route
King St
Bruce Trail
Bruce Trail
Twenty Mile Creek
Glen Rd
1 Cataract trail to Upper Balls Falls
2 Balls Falls
3 Historic Mill Site and Ball home
4 Stairs into valley /start of old-growth forest
5 Fork of Bruce Trail / lower valley
6 Bruce Trail road access (limited parking)
7 Jordan Hollow Park / picnic area
Sixth Ave
21st St
Balls Falls Conservation area
0
150
300 m
N
P

have the time, include a visit to the upper falls, the hamlet of Glen Elgin at Balls Falls, and Jordan Village, where you can get quality food and drinks, including wine tasting. The Jordan Historical Museum (at the Lincoln Cultural Centre) is particularly worthwhile. It could all be done in a return hike, but you may wish to drive to Jordan Village until a trail connection is completed to bypass the perilously narrow section of King Street. There are nine wineries on the Twenty Mile Bench landform, so a wine and old-growth forest tour is more than possible.

✣ Learn more

There is a lot of history around Twenty Valley and Jordan Valley; accounts of settlers date back more than 200 years, Indigenous Peoples for millennia before that. The area stands out for a local commitment to preserving its history, particularly that of the early settlers. In 1953 a museum was founded in Jordan Village to preserve items from the Mennonite community that settled in the area in 1799 after walking from Pennsylvania. In 2021, the museum moved to a modern building to house the collection, which includes unique Fraktur calligraphy and art dating back more than 200 years. There are many historic buildings in the village, dominated by an old cider and vinegar factory that now houses posh shops, restaurants, and a winery.

If you park at Balls Falls, you'll see a number of historic buildings, about half of which are original to the site, while the rest were moved there. The oldest original structures are a grist mill dating back to 1809, and a Georgian-style brick house which was built in 1846. Some buildings that have been moved to the property date back as far as 1800. The intention was to recreate the hamlet of Glen Elgin before it eventually faded away as the mills closed here and population growth moved below the escarpment.

The gorge below the falls is a beautiful walk, and includes a link of the Bruce Trail, but its recognition as an old-growth forest is relatively recent. In 2003, old-growth forest expert, Bruce Kershner, visited the gorge and counted annual growth rings on fallen logs that had been cut from the trail. He counted 325 rings on a sugar maple and over 300 rings on a hemlock, making this an exceptionally old forest for this part of Ontario. Many other tree species reach ages of over 200 years. To put that in perspective, when the first Europeans settled the area around 1780 (both Jordan Village and the ghost town of Glen Elgin), these trees were already over 100-years-old.

Starting at Balls Falls, to reach the stairs into the gorge, you'll walk through the pioneer village and toward the arboretum, climbing a short set of stairs before descending a much longer one into the valley. From the top of the stairs, you can already see old-growth trees growing on the steep valley slopes, particularly hemlock and sugar maple. The Bruce Trail leading down the gorge winds around some particularly old sugar maples that likely date back to the late 1600s. The old-growth forest continues nearly until the Bruce Trail leaves the valley to cross Glen Road.

This is a mixed age forest, and many of the old trees aren't especially large because they are growing on shallow, rocky soil, so this is a good place to look for other characteristics of old trees. These include bark balding, flaky or shaggy bark, staghorn-shaped crowns, moss-covered trunks, branches high on the tree (celery stalk shape), and buttressed trunks. The many scattered boulders are moss-covered with an attractive smattering of ferns, including rock cap fern and wood ferns. Between the boulders and fallen logs, dense mats of Canada yew add beauty to the understory. Yew can grow here for the same reason that the old-growth forest was left alone: the steep valley is hard to access. In the case of the old trees, it was too steep for lumbermen to haul trees out easily. In the case of the shrubby yew, the steep rocky valley is inhospitable to deer that would otherwise nibble away the new growth every winter.

As you reach the lower boundary of the old-growth forest, you have the option of continuing out of the valley on the Bruce Trail (the parking lot here on Glen Road could be an alternate starting point for your hike) or following a trail that stays close to the Creek and crosses under King Street to Jordan Hollow Park. From there it's a short walk to Jordan Village, but unfortunately it includes a short but treacherous section of King Street with no shoulder or walkway. In very low water you may be able to continue along the creek bed.

The area is renowned for its wines; the Twenty Mile Bench wine region has nine vineyards at the time of writing. Sheltered north-facing slopes and Lake Ontario breezes moderate the temperature year round, creating ideal growing conditions for many grapes, including Riesling, Pinot Noir, and Chardonnay.

A small pocket of mixed old-growth forest is found in the valley below Grimsby Point.

Grimsby Point (Beamer Memorial Conservation Area)

✤ What you'll like

Grimsby Point has long been famous for its spectacular lookout, and hawk watching during the spring migration. The large old oaks on the plateau, and a small pocket of old hemlock and maple forest in the ravine below also make this a worthy destination to see old-growth forest. There are two waterfalls, though neither ranks among the more scenic falls on the escarpment.

✤ How to get there

By car – Beamer Memorial can be reached in about an hour by car from downtown Toronto without traffic. The easiest access is the parking area on Quarry Road. Take exit 74 from the QEW (Regional Road 10/Casablanca Blvd), turn left on Main Street, right on Woolverton Road, and left on Ridge Rd. Watch for Quarry Road, signs for Beamer Memorial, on your left.

By public transit – From the Burlington GO station, transfer to bus #12 toward Niagara Falls, and get out at the Casablanca Park and Ride GO stop. The lower valley trailhead off Gibson Street (43.1916, -79.5652) can be reached on foot in a little under an hour, or you can use Niagara Region Transit OnDemand app, other ride sharing apps, or a taxi to reach the Gibson Street or Quarry Road trailheads.

By bike – The Greenbelt Cycle Route runs along Ridge Road W close to the Quarry Road parking, and the falls viewpoint parking. You could also bike from the GO stop or other places within the town of Grimsby to the Gibson Street trailhead.

✣ What to do

This is worth a visit almost anytime. If you're interested in hawks, visit during the spring with a good pair of binoculars. For fall colours, plan on late October, but this can vary quite a bit from year to year. If you're feeling energetic, start the hike from the valley bottom, combined with the loop on the plateau. If you aren't up for a vigorous climb, or are pressed for time, the old growth is mostly on the plateau, so you'll want to opt for the trailhead at Quarry Road instead. There are restaurants, cafés, and pubs along Main Street W, east of Mountain Street, which is only a short walk from the Gibson Street trailhead.

✣ Learn more

It's a rare delight to walk with someone who has a deep abiding connection to a place, particularly one that spans generations. In writing this book, it happened to me at Peter's Woods, and here at Grimsby Point. Standing in the forest, looking at a large patch of periwinkle in the forest with Bruce Mackenzie, I only later realized that it was likely Mackenzie's great-grandmother, Gertrude Metcalfe, who planted it in the 1920s. The periwinkle once grew by a now-vanished tearoom that stood on the edge of what was (even then) an old-growth forest. The laneway to the tea house ran near the existing trail on the west side of the creek. The house where Gertrude Metcalfe (née Beamer) lived is now a bed and breakfast and retreat centre.

The Point Woods, as it was then called, made a cameo appearance in the life of Harry Oakes, a millionaire whose unsolved murder in the Bahamas was the subject of a 2019 book. Oakes bought the property from the Metcalfes and owned it until his mysterious death in 1943. During that time, Gertrude Metcalfe ran the tearoom in partnership with Oakes. High-profile guests included actors Randolph Scott and Will Rogers. All that remains today is the barely discernible foundation, the remnants of a bridge over a small creek, and the periwinkle.

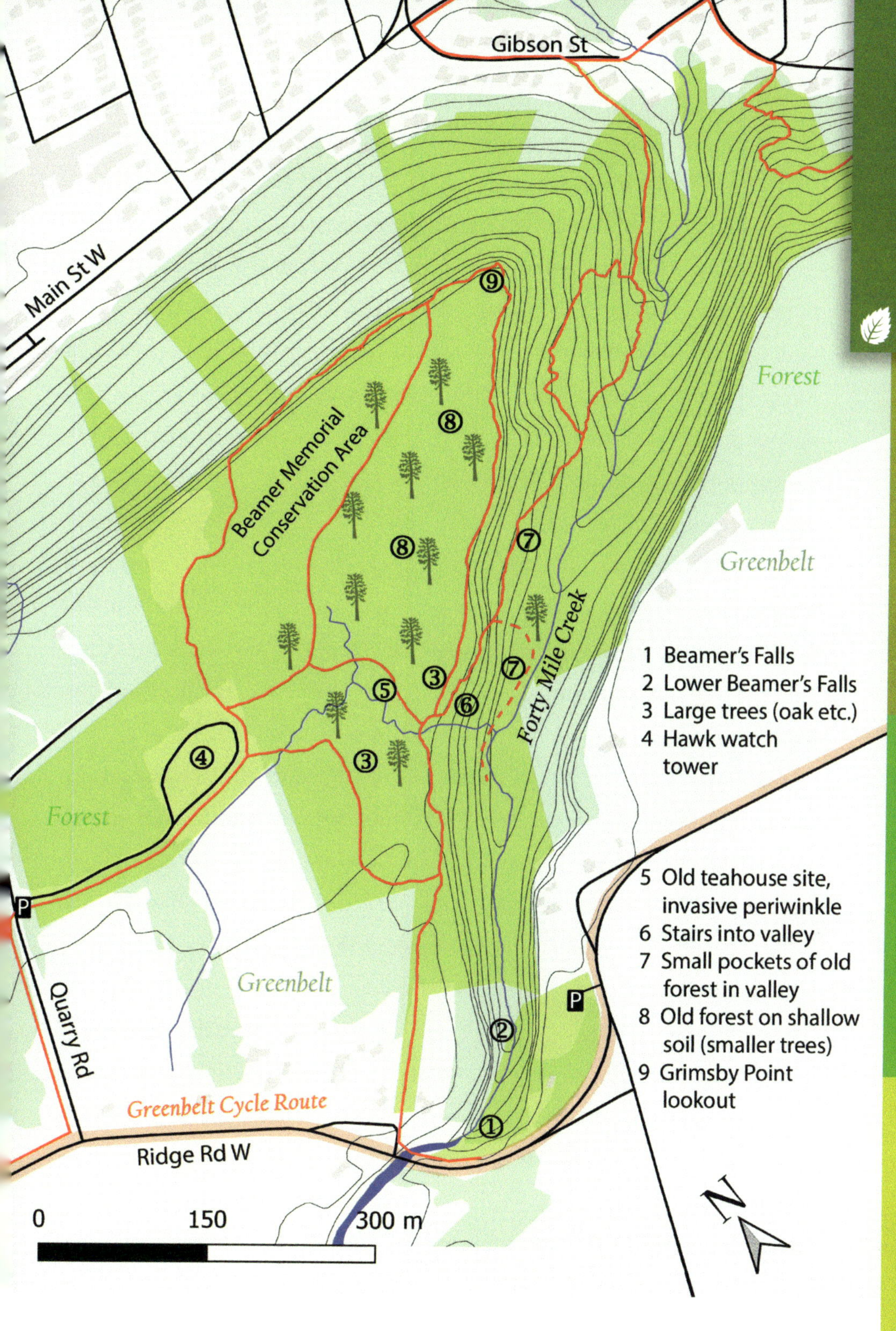
Gibson St
Main St W
Beamer Memorial Conservation Area
Forest
Greenbelt
Forty Mile Creek
Forest
Greenbelt
Quarry Rd
Greenbelt Cycle Route
Ridge Rd W
P
P
0
150
300 m
N
1 Beamer's Falls
2 Lower Beamer's Falls
3 Large trees (oak etc.)
4 Hawk watch tower
5 Old teahouse site, invasive periwinkle
6 Stairs into valley
7 Small pockets of old forest in valley
8 Old forest on shallow soil (smaller trees)
9 Grimsby Point lookout

Our talk turned back to the periwinkle, an invasive plant about which Mackenzie didn't seem overly concerned, until I pointed out the relentless slow spread of the plant, which I'd seen firsthand at Eaton Hall. We looked at how far the patch already extended, and he started to rethink his opinion.

The forest is quite spectacular, with trees reaching around 300 years in age although most of the woods are on rather thin soil and the trees are understated, particularly closer to the viewpoint. Some of the most spectacular forest is in the general vicinity of the old tearoom, where the soils are deep enough for the trees to get big, and just before the edge of old farm fields. Centuries-old white oak, sugar maple, bitternut hickory, and an impressive red maple can all be found there.

You'd be forgiven for thinking the forest close to the point wasn't old growth at all; the trees are certainly quite average in size. But look up, and large, twisting branches suggest otherwise. Then look down and you'll see that the trees are standing on shelves of rock, their roots tracing the edges in the thin soil; a good clue as to why the trees grow slowly.

Grimsby Point was one of the forests identified by Bruce Kershner, an old-growth researcher from New York State, who inventoried old growth throughout the Niagara Peninsula in the early 2000s. He was effusive not only about the impressive Carolinian forest on the plateau, but also the ancient cedars growing on the cliffs and along the rim. Since the trail follows the rim closely, you'll be walking along the edge of the ancient cedar "forest." The oldest trees are growing out of sight on the cliff face itself, but some of the diminutive cedars along the interface of cliff and trail may be as old as the forest giants nearby. The Cliff Ecology Research Group at the University of Guelph surveyed some of the cedars on the cliffs, and the oldest they found would be around 300-years-old today. If there aren't any older ones, it may be that the rock of the cliff here is too unstable to support them longer than a few centuries.

Cedars along the escarpment edge are often older than they look.

The view from Grimsby Point.

Trees, be they cedars or oaks, aren't what Beamer Memorial Conservation Area is best known for. It is famous for hawk watching during the spring migration. For more than 40 years, volunteers have been gathering at Beamer Memorial every spring to count raptors as they pass through. The long timeline and the significant concentration of hawks in one place make Grimsby Point one of North America's most significant raptor migration monitoring sites. But why do hawks concentrate on this one spot? Probably you've watched a hawk soar seemingly effortlessly, tracing lazy circles through the sky. The large birds use thermals, columns of warm air, to give them lift. Because thermals don't tend to form over water, during spring migration, raptors are forced to go around the Great Lakes, which effectively funnels them into the Niagara peninsula (among other places).

The escarpment creates another type of air current, as winds hit the cliff face and create updrafts that hawks can also ride. Grimsby is special in a couple of ways: it is where the escarpment comes closest to the Lake Ontario shoreline, and it is one of the highest points on the escarpment, relative to the plain below. Starting in March, raptors can be seen soaring over Grimsby Point on updrafts early in the day, then using thermals that form over nearby farmlands later in the afternoon. The best time to go is mid-April to mid-May, 10 AM to 2 PM. On Good Friday each year, Niagara Peninsula Hawkwatch organizes an open house at Grimsby Point, with public events to learn more about the raptor migration.

Niagara escarpment Central/North

McMaster Forest

✤ What you'll like

Nestled within the city of Hamilton, McMaster Forest offers an enjoyable walk through restored tallgrass prairie to one of the finest old-growth forest pockets in southern Ontario. Carolinian tree species, including tulip tree and Sassafras, reach good sizes. Other parts of the forest are dominated by shade-tolerant sugar maple and hemlock, and scattered white pines emerge through the canopy. This is not one to miss!

✤ How to get there

By car – The forest is easily reached by car and there are parking spots at the trailhead on Lower Lion's Club Road, near Wilson Street E (43.2446, -79.9525).

By public transit – The closest bus stop is the West Hamilton Bus Loop and then a short walk to the forest down Lower Lions Club Road.

By bike – The Hamilton–Brantford Rail Trail crosses Main Street only two kilometres from the trailhead. Bike up Main Street and Wilson to get there. The Rail Trail joins the Greenbelt Cycle Route to the west.

A large bur oak shows there was likely savannah forest here in the past.

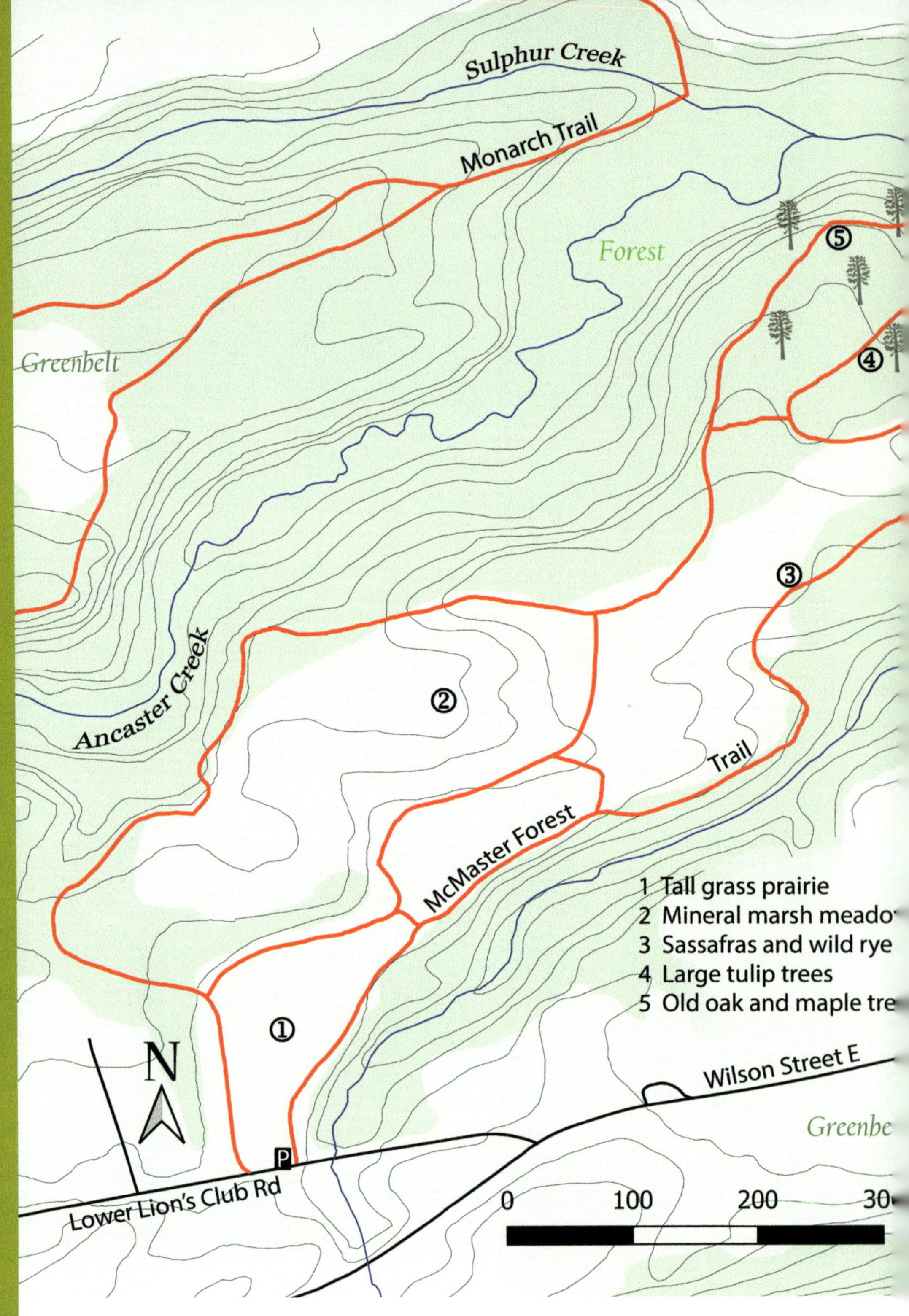
Sulphur Creek
Monarch Trail
Forest
Greenbelt
Ancaster Creek
McMaster Forest
Trail
1 Tall grass prairie
2 Mineral marsh meado
3 Sassafras and wild rye
4 Large tulip trees
5 Old oak and maple tre
N
P
Lower Lion's Club Rd
Wilson Street E
Greenbe
0
100
200
30

✤ What to do

Plan to spend a couple of hours exploring the trail system through the prairie and forest. Turn on a GPS to help orient yourself on the trail system, which at times can be quite vague. For further hiking, there are extensive trails in adjacent Dundas Valley Conservation Area, or you could visit Beamer Memorial Conservation Area in Grimsby.

✤ Learn more

On a visit to McMaster Forest in 2012, Wayne Terryberry found himself wading through dense thickets of European buckthorn, a highly invasive shrub that is notoriously hard to get rid of. What a mess, he thought to himself. But he could see possibilities in the site. Terryberry is the Coordinator of Outdoor Recreation and Natural Lands for McMaster University, which has owned the land since 1964. Not far from the field of buckthorn was an astonishingly intact (some say untouched) old-growth forest. I think it's likely that the old-growth forest now found at McMaster Forest was at least selectively logged around the time of settlement, around 220 years ago, but certainly this is among the least disturbed forests in the region, and may have trees that predate settlement.

The land was farmed by several families from the late 1700s until 1954. From 1888 to 1954, the land was owned by the McMullen family, and it is largely thanks to this family that we have an old-growth forest today. Assuming there was some logging at settlement when they bought the farm, the forest might have been about 100-years-old, more or less. Over the next few decades, it would have matured to the point of having quite a bit of valuable timber, but for whatever reason (They enjoyed the forest? They weren't interested in timber? They were too busy growing potatoes?), the family refrained from significant logging in the forest for the next 66 years.

After Ernest McMullen sold the property in 1954, it changed hands a few times until McMaster University bought the property in 1964, intending to develop it and build a connecting road to the main campus along Ancaster Creek. The purchase was a happy mistake by the University, which quickly learned why the site had kept changing hands. Heavy clay soil and poor drainage made development impractical. The land languished for the next four decades, and the University administration largely forgot that it even owned the land.

The University's hands-off approach during this time might have been a good thing for the old-growth forest overlooking Ancaster Creek. "Managing" forests in southern Ontario too often meant logging them during the 1980s. The old fields degenerated into a tangle of invasive species, with little value for wildlife.

As you walk into McMaster Forest today, you begin your hike in a tallgrass prairie dominated by Indian grass mixed with big bluestem, switchgrass, and wild rye. "I'm just amazed to go there now and see the prairie," says Terryberry, recalling his first visits when the site was a tangle of buckthorn as far as he could see. The amazing transition didn't happen overnight.

First the buckthorn was cut and burned from what had once been Ernest McMullen's potato fields. Buckthorn is notoriously hard to get rid of because it resprouts from the roots, so the larger cut stems were treated with herbicides while the smaller shrubs were pulled out, roots and all. Any regrowth was killed off when the site was intentionally burned.

Then the grasses were planted and allowed to spread. The prairie ecosystem is beautiful, especially in late summer and autumn when the grasses are flowering and going to seed. It is maintained by prescribed burns every few years, as well as occasional visits by goats, which are part of Terryberry's private herd.

Goats are ideal because they love to eat woody stems, and the young regrowing shoots of buckthorn were a delicious treat for them. Because

Canada wild rye grows around the edges of the restored prairie at McMaster Forest.

goats are browsers (that eat woody stems) and not grazers (that eat grass and herbs), they have helped continue the work of buckthorn control after the planting of native prairie grasses, but the most important control on invasive shrubs are the periodic prescribed burns.

Why go to all the trouble to make a field of grass, as pretty as it is? Ontario is a forest province and has been for millennia. Before European colonization a few centuries ago, there was also a lot more prairie and savannah dotted on the landscape, mixed in with the dense shady forest we usually think of. It was maintained in part by fires that were intentionally (and sometimes accidentally) set to maintain hunting grounds around First Nations settlements. As the acclaimed ecologist, John Riley, puts it, "Where there had been Native nations, there had been grasslands."

Savannah and tallgrass prairie are unique habitat for a variety of plants (like the blazing star), insects (such as the Karner blue butterfly), and wildlife (like the northern bobwhite), but today, they are among the rarest

of ecosystems in Ontario. Projects like the one at McMaster Forest are gradually bringing them back.

Since prairie and savannah tended to be associated with Indigenous occupation, it's fitting to restore it at McMaster Forest. Indigenous trails were arguably found nearly everywhere in southern Ontario, but due to quirks of geology and geography, the Dundas Valley was a particularly important travel route.

The Dundas Valley was at one time a massive river gorge, even larger than the one below Niagara Falls today. The equivalent waterfall would have been near Copetown. The advance and retreat of glaciers over millennia pushed glacial till (a mix of everything from clay to boulders) into the valley, filling it 200 metres deep. What was once an impassable gorge and waterfall became the relatively gentle slope of the Dundas Valley, making it a natural place for a trail over the Niagara Escarpment.

In fact, if you wanted to get from Lake Ontario to Lake Erie, the "Head of the Lake" portage (or carrying place) up the Dundas Valley to the Grand River was one of the easiest ways to do it. Easy was relative. The Head of the Lake portage, at over 40 km, won't be making a comeback with modern canoe trippers anytime soon. But as Bob Henderson points out in his book, *Every Trail has a Story*, one early translation for the name of the competing Niagara Gorge portage was "crawling on all fours." Enough said.

Meanwhile, if you wanted to get to Lake St. Clair, and thence to Lake Huron, the Head of the Lake portage continued to the headwaters of the Thames River, near Woodstock, allowing you to bypass Lake Erie altogether. In much the same way that Toronto was founded at the base of the Carrying Place Trail, Dundas (the Head of the Lake) was founded at the base of this important Indigenous travel route. It was one of the first areas in Ontario to be settled by the British.

About a kilometre and a half from McMaster's restored prairie is Governor's Road, which was one of the first roads built by the British in Upper Canada. It was designed to parallel the route of the ancient trail over the escarpment to the Grand River and then (as Hwy 2) all the way to the Thames River at Woodstock. Although at times they would have followed the same route, the Head of the Lake Portage respected the natural topography more than British roads did. It might have followed parts of the Spring Creek Trail and Hamilton–Brantford Rail Trail, and/or the Heritage Trail and Powerline Trail.

But as the French say, my head is in the moon. Let's come back to earth and continue our walk through McMaster Forest. After the tallgrass prairie you'll walk through patches of wild rye growing in the open and under young trees and shrubs, before walking under the tall canopy of the old-growth forest. What struck me about McMaster Forest was both the diversity of tree species and their size.

The east and south side of the old growth has typical Carolinian Ontario tree species, like walnut and tulip trees, that are impressively large. Tulip trees along the trail reach over a metre in diameter. These are trees that need a little more sun to grow, and have thrived here near the edges of old farm fields. Historic logging may have helped them get started, or perhaps they got started in open savannah forest.

Along the east and north side of the hill overlooking Ancaster Creek, shade-loving trees like maple, beech, and hemlock thrive. Some of the maples have big branches high up the tree, and bark balding at the base of the trunk, that show their age. There are also some old white pines and oaks, which again may have gotten their start during early logging some 200-odd years ago, or before that in savannah forest. The view from here across the valley when the leaves are down may have looked over the Head of the Lake portage, and this dry lookout in McMaster Forest might have been an attractive spot for occasional encampments over the millennia.

I can't say whether Wayne Terryberry and others are right that this is a virgin old-growth forest that has never been logged, but I can easily believe the forest was never completely cleared—making it very special and rare. It feels that way, and you don't need to be a seasoned ecologist to pick up on it.

Rattlesnake Point and Crawford Lake Conservation Areas

✤ What you'll like

Rattlesnake point is one of the best places along the Niagara Escarpment to access the bottom of the cliff and see ancient cedars. Some eastern white cedars growing on the cliff face reach up to 600-years-old, with many others measuring their age in centuries. The hike between Rattlesnake Point and Crawford Lake also leads past a number of impressive lookouts, and through a nice shady maple-dominated forest that is approaching the old-growth stage.

A boardwalk trail circles Crawford Lake through an old-growth forest of relatively small cedars in the fragmented limestone bedrock. At nearby reconstructions of longhouses, you'll learn about the village and the people who lived there 600 years ago.

✤ How to get there

By car – From Highway 401, exit at Guelph Line and follow it southeast (toward Burlington) about four kilometres to the entrance of Crawford Lake Conservation Area. Or to reach Rattlesnake Point, turn left on Limestone Road, right on Appleby Line, and drive roughly four kilometres to the entrance.

By public transit – There is no direct public transit to the Conservation Areas. However, they are close to Milton, so it is possible to use a taxi/ride service, bike, or even take a long walk from the Milton GO station.

Depending on the schedule, GO trains are the fastest way to travel between Toronto and Milton (about one hour). GO bus #21 also leaves from the Union Station Bus terminal and takes between 1:10 and 1:40 to reach the Milton GO station, depending on time of day.

By bike – It's about a 40-minute bike ride from the Milton GO station to the entrance of Rattlesnake Point, or about a one and a half to two-hour bike

Ancient cedars at Rattlesnake Point Conservation Area

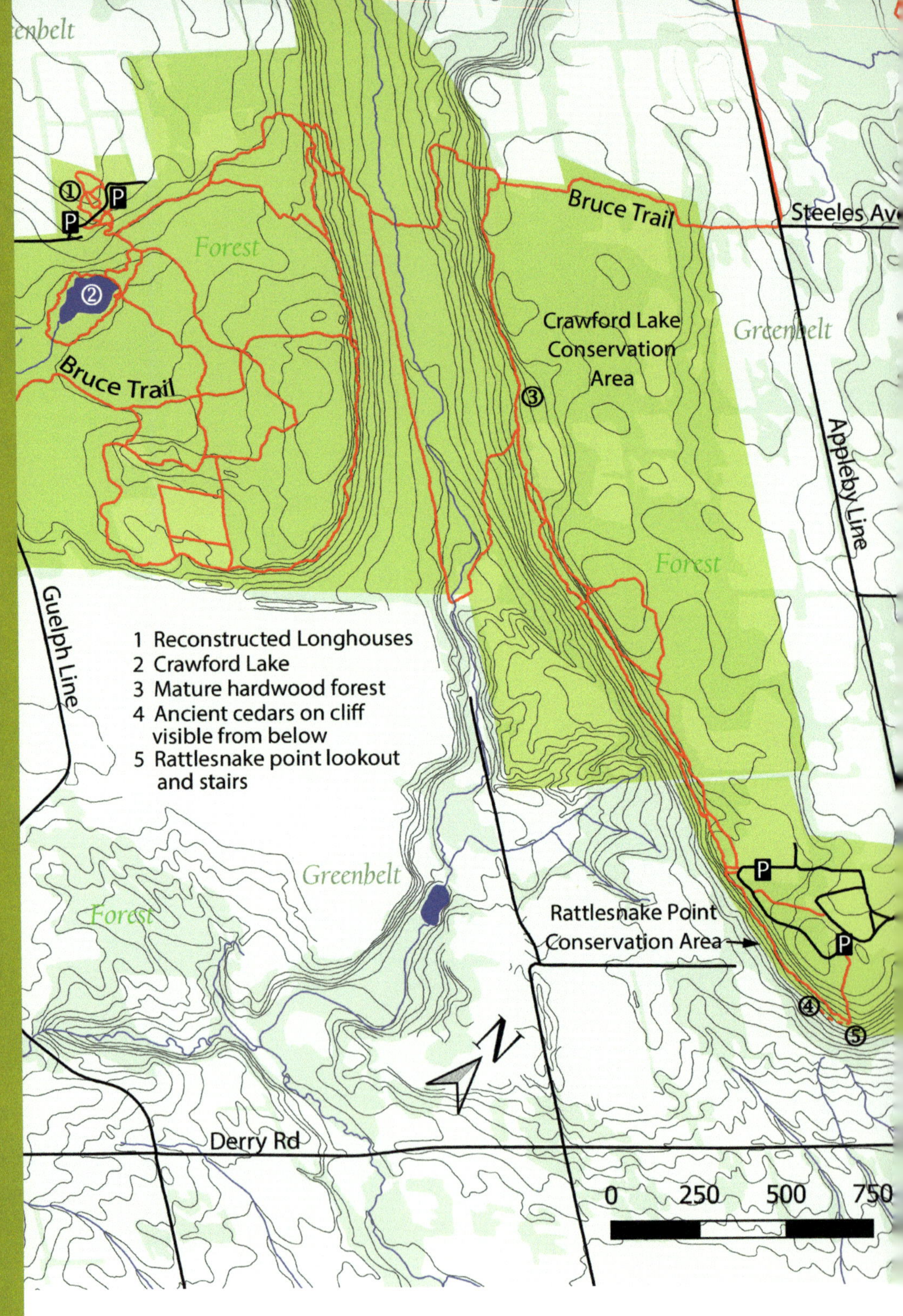
Greenbelt
Bruce Trail
Steeles Av
Forest
Crawford Lake
Conservation
Area
Greenbelt
Bruce Trail
Appleby Line
Forest
Guelph Line
1 Reconstructed Longhouses
2 Crawford Lake
3 Mature hardwood forest
4 Ancient cedars on cliff
visible from below
5 Rattlesnake point lookout
and stairs
Greenbelt
Forest
Rattlesnake Point
Conservation Area
N
Derry Rd
0
250
500
750

ride from Burlington or Oakville. The Greenbelt cycle route runs about 3 km SW of Crawford Lake.

✣ What to do

Both Rattlesnake point and Crawford Lake are worth a visit. If you're feeling energetic and can spare four to five hours for a round trip, you should consider hiking the connecting trail. Or you can go see the ancient cedars at Rattlesnake point (hike to the lookout, descend the stairs, and walk west along the base of the cliff), then drive to Crawford Lake. Either way, you may want to plan your lunch stop at Rattlesnake Point, as it is usually less crowded, or find a restaurant in Milton.

✣ Learn more

When I visited Crawford Lake Conservation Area, it felt overrun with tourists, which is often the case for this popular spot. I'm also a tourist, of course—usually that wouldn't stop me from being irrationally annoyed at the crowds, but here I can't bring myself to do it. There's simply too much to enjoy about this place. Crawford Lake is a beautiful, enigmatic lake that sits like an emerald atop the crown of the Niagara Escarpment. Thousands of years ago an underground river flowed here, draining glacial meltwater through the limestone bedrock. At some point, a small section of rock over the river caved in, blocking the flow and creating an unusually deep, small lake atop the Niagara Escarpment. At least, that's one theory for how Crawford Lake formed. However it formed, it's an unusual lake.

In the late 1960s, scientists realized there was something very special about Crawford Lake. In most of Canada's lakes the water at the bottom holds steady at around four degrees Celsius, the temperature at which water is most dense. This cold water layer doesn't usually mix with the warmer water above—except for twice a year, in spring and fall, when the surface water also reaches about four degrees. Then a windy day will cause the whole lake to mix, carrying oxygen-rich surface water to the lake bottom, making life possible in the deepest parts of the lake. In very rare lakes, the surface water never mixes with the water at the bottom of the lake. These are called meromictic lakes, and they are invariably small but deep lakes. Crawford Lake is one of only twelve known meromictic lakes in Canada.

At the bottom of every meromictic lake is a band of cold, oxygen-deprived water that is never disturbed by the currents at the lake's surface, or by fish or mussels digging in the mud (since most animal life can't exist without oxygen). Anything that sinks to the bottom of the lake is nearly perfectly preserved in place. Sure, it's a bit creepy; it can also be very useful. Layers of sediment at the bottom of Crawford Lake alternate in colour—dissolved limestone precipitates out in summer, creating light layers; organic matter settles out in winter to make dark layers. So, each pair of bands represents one year of deposition, and trapped within the sediments are grains of pollen that blew into the lake from surrounding plants. The result is more than 700 years of annual vegetation change that a skilled paleoecologist can read.

In the early 1970s, scientists started doing just that, with the intention of reconstructing past climate for this part of North America. They found that the lake was surrounded by a fairly typical beech maple forest until around the year 1500, at which point they noted a shift to oak–pine forest. They also started finding pollen from maize (corn) in the samples between 1310 and 1535 AD. This was particularly exciting because pollen from maize is heavy and rarely blows more than a kilometre.

The obvious inference was that there had been an Indigenous settlement nearby, and by 1972, remnants of an Iroquoian village (probably Wendat or Neutral) was found half a kilometre from the lake. Skip forward to today.When you visit Crawford Lake you can see reconstructions of the original longhouses that were once found at this site.

Standing among the impressive longhouses at Crawford Lake today, you can imagine the village that stood for around two decades between 1436 and 1457. This same village site was occupied at least one other time, and other village sites were established within a few kilometres of Crawford Lake. The longhouses are bigger than those of my imagination, but as impressive as they are, it was only later that I realized the true significance of this site.

It's amazing that this village site was located and (more or less) accurately reconstructed based on the old post holes found on the site. But this village reconstruction only hints at the many, many sites that were widely scattered across southern Ontario, part of a widespread agricultural society composed of many Nations within several Confederacies. Wendat, Neutral, and Haudenosaunee villages were temporary, moving from place to place every few decades as soils were depleted. Environmental historian, George William Colpitts, points out the compelling irony that the reconstructed longhouses that were first built in the 1980s at Crawford Lake have now likely stood longer than the original village they represent.

From Crawford Lake it is about a two-hour hike across Nassagaweya Canyon, then along the escarpment to Rattlesnake Point. This hike leads through a continuous hardwood forest, all of which has been logged over the past two centuries (but some of the forest is once again approaching the old-growth stage). Standing at the Rattlesnake Point lookout, it's easy to imagine an Indigenous hunter pausing to look out from the dramatic viewpoint almost 600 years ago. Young cedar trees grow on the cliff beneath his feet. A hawk wheels on an updraft over the unbroken forest cover below. How could he imagine the changes that would be wrought on that landscape over the ensuing centuries—or the alliances, the broken promises, the tragedies still many years in the future. He turns and walks back into the woods to hunt for deer.

The oldest cedars at Rattlesnake Point have been growing there for over 600 years. When Indigenous people were first clearing land for agriculture, and building longhouses near Crawford Lake, a tiny eastern white cedar seedling was growing on a ledge of the cliff below Rattlesnake Point, its roots creeping into small fissures in the rock to find a dependable source of water and nutrients. It continued to grow, defying the odds for centuries as villages came and went, and came and went again. Europeans started settling the land nearby, including Henry Stingle in 1845, and Murray Crawford who

A reconstructed fifteenth-century longhouse at Crawford Lake.

built a cottage at Crawford Lake in 1899. Murray Crawford bought the land so he could cut the timber for his sawmill. He was probably especially interested in the oak and pine that had started growing on former Iroquoian farm fields and village sites in the 1500s.

When the longhouse site was discovered in 1972, our humble cedar plugged away in obscurity, growing so slowly each year that it was barely discernible. In the late 1980s a group of scientists stood near the cliff-top at Rattlesnake Point. They were intending to form a research group that focused on the cliff ecosystem, and they pondered the transition from shady maple forest to sparse cedars to cliff face (most ecologists seem to have a fascination with ecosystem boundaries). They thought, as everyone did at the time, that the small cedars were young trees, and wondered why they were growing there. Someone even speculated that maybe they had been planted.

It would be a couple of years before they would accidentally discover the truth. Doug Larson, lead scientist of the nascent Cliff Ecology Research Group at the University of Guelph, was out on his first day with their high school intern, Ceddy Nash. They were surveying cliff edges near Milton to determine the effects of hiking trails on the forest near the cliff edge. They needed to understand the age structure of the forest, they assumed the smaller trees were younger, but they wanted to know how much younger. So, they borrowed a tree corer (a hollow drill bit that let them extract a pencil-shaped piece of wood to count the annual growth rings) and set out to age some trees.

When they withdrew the first tree cores from cedars near the cliff edge, it was hard to see the rings. Larson concluded he would need to bring the samples home, glue them in place, and sand them to see the rings clearly. When he did that, what he saw kept him awake that night, and the next. Four hundred years. That was the age of the trees they had assumed were no more than 50-years-old!

The effects of hiking were now an afterthought, and by the end of that summer they had ring counts over 500 years, and estimated ages over 700 years. Over the next few summers, rock climbers, Pete Kelly and Cal Clark, would climb cliffs up and down the Niagara Escarpment, and they would confirm that the discoveries near Milton were commonplace, and were actually eclipsed by the discovery of many trees that were over 1,000-years-old!

The initial discovery of the ancient cedars occurred in one of the most populated parts of Canada, after two centuries of European settlement. How were they overlooked for so long? They had no commercial value, and they didn't fit our preconceptions. We didn't see them because we didn't believe they were there. What's maybe even more surprising is that people have lived alongside ancient trees without realizing it in many disparate parts of the world. In 1997, Doug Larson used a sabbatical to visit many places in Europe and the United States and found, in nearly every case, the oldest known tree in that country or state.

These ancient trees are found in seemingly the most inhospitable places because they are left alone. They're safe from animals, people, fire, and competition. Water flowing through the cracks where they are rooted is often very dependable—but the cracks put an upper limit on the mass of roots, and so the trees often remain very small (to learn more about recognizing ancient cedars, see Horse Lake and Flowerpot Island).

Although it doesn't have the oldest ancient cedars on the escarpment, Rattlesnake Point is special because it's one of the easiest places to get to the bottom of the escarpment and get a good look at them. For obvious reasons, it's difficult for anyone but rock climbers to get close to many of the ancient cedars on the cliff face. But at least you can use the stairs at Rattlesnake Point to descend to the base of the cliff, and the rough climber's trail to walk along the base, to a view where a number of ancient cedars are visible, commonly reaching a few centuries old.

At the end of the day, I hiked back to Crawford Lake. New research has begun that uses the sediment layers to examine the past, but in this case, it also has implications for the future. Crawford Lake is one of a dozen sites around the planet where researchers have identified distinct markers for the start of the Anthropocene, an as yet unofficial epoch in the geologic timescale.

The Anthropocene indicates the era in which humans began to have a significant influence on the climate and ecology of the planet, to the point where it will be captured in the rock strata. It's not clear if or when this will be adopted as an official unit in geologic time. But it should be—it's

The aquamarine Crawford Lake holds many secrets, including centuries of human occupation and the beginning of the Anthropocene Epoch.

undeniable that humans are a dominant force in shaping life and climate on planet earth (and I think the sooner we accept we have responsibility and agency the better, for us and all life on this planet). The question of when exactly this theoretical epoch began is the subject of research at Crawford Lake, among other places. The most likely markers are nuclear isotopes from atomic bomb testing, but mercury, microplastics, and fly ash are all possibilities.

I'm reminded of something Doug Larson said to me when I interviewed him about ancient cedars over a decade ago. Toward the end of the interview, I mentioned how exciting it must be to be studying such old organisms. Yes, he said, but it also sometimes fills him with a sense of dread. "People have trouble even with a five-year planning window," he said. "I'd like to think that we should have a planning window that includes one generation of the forest that I'm working on. That's a thousand years ... It fills me with a sense of hope alternating with dread when I look at this forest, because I just don't know if we're going to be good enough stewards of our environment generally to allow one more ancient generation to develop."

Scotsdale Farm

✤ What you'll like

Scotsdale Farm is part of a large intact natural area with potential for days of explorations. Start off at a historic farmhouse and barn, then walk down the laneway to an impressive 200-year-old sugar maple–beech forest, followed up by a 300-year-old hemlock and white cedar swamp forest. Top it off with streams, waterfalls, and boardwalks connected to endless hiking on the Bruce Trail and in adjacent conservation areas.

✤ How to get there

By car – Scotsdale Farm is within an hour of Toronto or Hamilton, and only minutes from Georgetown by car. The parking at Scotsdale (43.687, -79.991) is free and close to the old-growth forest. Other parking is available in Silver Creek Conservation Area and at roadside locations.

By public transit – There is no direct transit to the forest, but there is regular GO bus service to Georgetown. From there you can bike or use a taxi to get to the forest. Alternately you could walk from the GO station to the closest trailheads in Silver Creek Conservation Area in an hour and a half (or less), a lot of it on Eighth Line, a pleasant but narrow country road.

By bike – Scotsdale Farm can be reached by bicycle in about half an hour from the Georgetown GO station. The Greenbelt Cycle Route runs within four kilometres of the trailhead on Eighth Line, or about the same to the main entrance on much busier Trafalgar Road.

✤ What to do

The most impressive old-growth forest can be experienced in a one-to-two-hour hike, but if you have more time, continue into Silver Creek Conservation Area and walk a loop. Bring a GPS or use your phone, as the trails can be

Old-growth sugar maple forest along the Bruce Trail

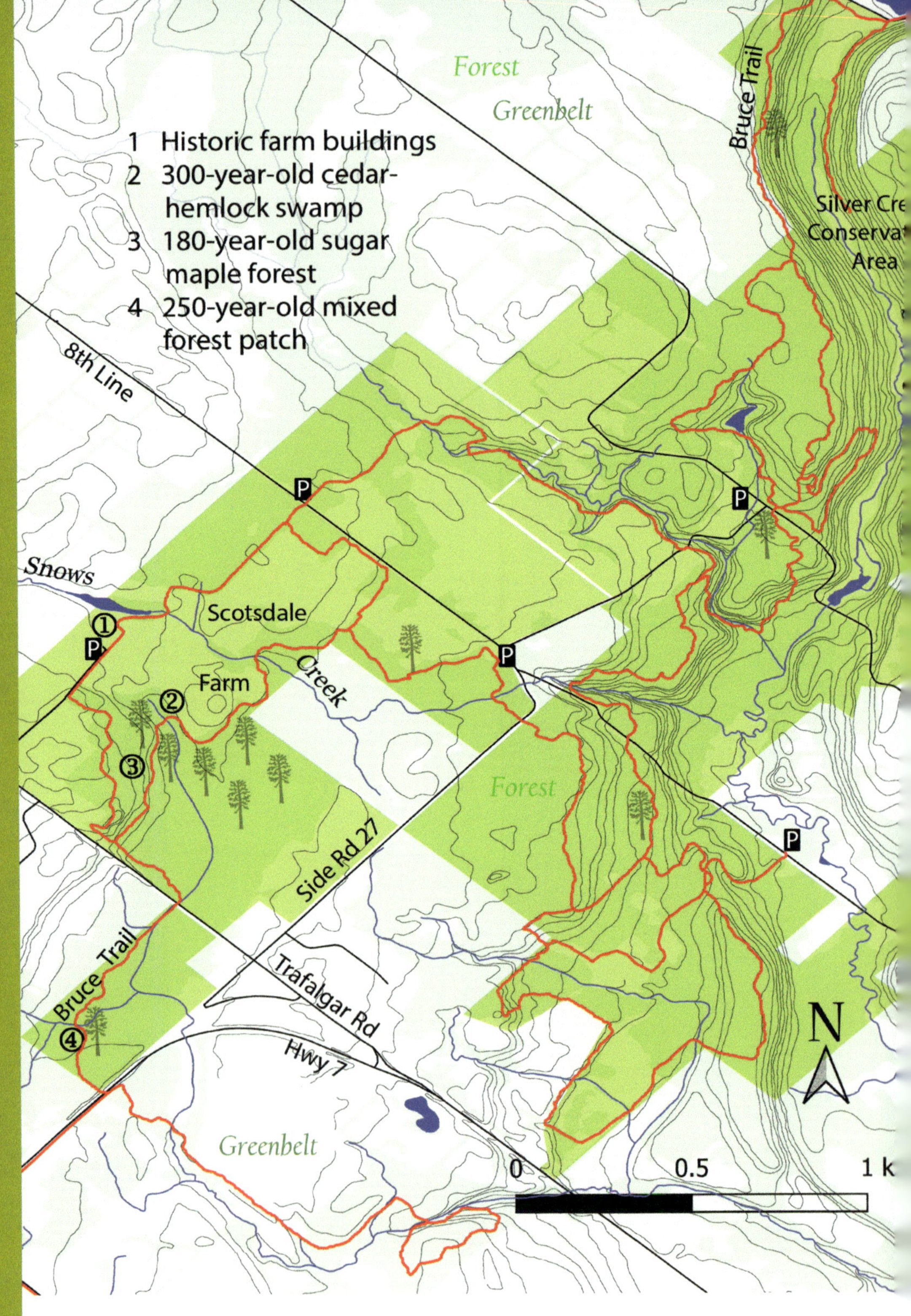

1 Historic farm buildings
2 300-year-old cedar-hemlock swamp
3 180-year-old sugar maple forest
4 250-year-old mixed forest patch
Forest
Greenbelt
Bruce Trail
Silver Cre
Conserva
Area
8th Line
Snows
Scotsdale
Farm
Creek
Forest
Side Rd 27
Bruce Trail
Trafalgar Rd
Hwy 7
Greenbelt
N
0
0.5
1 k

confusing. You can hike as far as you like in Silver Creek and Terra Cotta Conservation Areas, or on the Bruce Trail.

✤ Learn more

Scotsdale Farm was a delightful surprise. I was just looking for convenient parking for sections of the Bruce Trail when I stumbled on it and realized it was a little-known haven for old-growth forest. Stewart and Letty Bennett bequeathed the farm to the Ontario Heritage Trust in 1982. When the Bennetts bought the historic Cooke farm in 1938, the maple–beech woodlot along Trafalgar Road was over 100-years-old. It had been logged around the time of settlement in the 1800s, and then left to grow back, but some trees dated back as far as the late 1700s. If anyone but wealthy hobby farmers had bought the land, I might not be writing about it today, but thanks to the Bennetts, it was largely left alone for the next 50 years. Stewart Bennett's wealth came in part from a family lumber business that had sawmills in northern Ontario, and he became president of Beardmore & Co. (which was one of Canada's oldest and largest leather manufacturers).

Ironically, some of the old-growth forest was selectively logged in 1991 after the property was donated to the Ontario Heritage Trust, despite opposition from conservationists. Some beech trees that were cut were over 200-years-old at the time. You can find a quietly outraged article about it online in the archives of Ontario Nature (then Seasons magazine). Neighbours of the farm told the author that "the Bennetts barely touched the trees on the old-growth part of their land, and were so concerned about protection that they spent thousands of dollars saving a single tree in one of their fields." Why the Ontario Heritage Foundation and Credit Valley Conservation thought it was a good idea to log it, knowing it was old-growth forest, is hard to fathom. It's a reminder that centuries of management can be undone with one bad decision, and financial incentives often point us astray. In that context, it's amazing and wonderful there's any old growth left in Southern Ontario at all! I don't think the logging of Scotsdale that began in 1991 was ever completed after a seasonal pause, so maybe the outrage of conservationists had some effect.

The parking for Scotsdale Farm is near the historic farmhouse and barns. The Bennetts renovated the pioneer farmhouse in 1938, leaving few outward signs of the original building encased within. One of the barns is also an original Cooke family barn. To reach the old growth from here, walk back down the lane you drove in on, then cut to the left on the Bennett Heritage Trail just inside the edge of the woods. At first, the forest is a mix of plantation and younger maple forest, but a large sugar maple with a ropey base and a trail blaze soon welcomes you to the old growth. Until recently this was a sugar maple–beech forest, with some ash mixed in, but most of the ash and beech have died from invasive emerald ash borer and beech bark disease. One fairly healthy beech tree that may be resistant is hidden in shrubs just off the trail (43.6834, -79.9904). Hopefully this tree will be a seed source for beech trees to one day recover in this forest (read more about beech, and disease-resistant trees at Bronte Creek, page 139). When the trail meets the junction of the Bruce Trail, walking either way will lead you to some old-growth forest, but the closest and most impressive old growth is to the left at the intersection.

A thicket of young Norway maple welcomes you on this trail branch, and I wonder how it even got there. I suppose someone planted one of these invasive trees near the roadside and it seeded into the gap. I hope someone will bring a tree-puller and a chainsaw and get them out before they grow into mature trees and spread further through the forest. The trouble with Norway maple is that its seeds aren't palatable to wildlife and its leaves are poor food for insects, so it has a competitive advantage over sugar maple, at the cost of mammals, insects, and birds. As Norway maple invades a

This sugar maple has signs of old age, including a sinuous trunk and sparse, large upper branches.

This boardwalk crosses through 300-year-old cedar–hemlock swamp forest, but the trees are diminutive.

forest, fewer and fewer other species can live there. It looks similar to the native sugar maple, but its toxic latex makes it very different indeed, and Canadian forests dominated by Norway maple have a relatively "silent spring." Ironically, Norway maple isn't even from Norway, rather it's from somewhere in central-eastern Europe, where other species in the ecosystem had millennia to adapt to its toxicity.

Thankfully the trail soon leads along the edge of an exceptional 200-year-old sugar maple forest. The trees aren't necessarily huge, but they have all the markers of age such as bark balding, ropey bases, sinuous trunks, and large upper branches—in short, they have character.

You'll walk through this forest for a while, then when the trail turns and crosses a swamp forest of small hemlock and white cedar trees, you may think you're leaving the old-growth forest behind. In fact, you've just entered the oldest forest on the Scotsdale property, with small hemlock and cedars that reach 250-to 300-years-old. Again, the trees have character, with twisty trunks/branches, and dead tops, but they are otherwise very small and unimpressive. A boardwalk across the swamp literally winds between 200-to 300-year-old trees, but thousands of people have walked it totally unaware of this fact. So, pause a moment, marvel at the mossy understory, charismatic dwarfed trees, and the serenity of this overlooked spot.

From here the trail follows the edge of the swamp, where more old trees can be seen, and a field full of milkweed. Since milkweeds are the only food source of monarch caterpillars, these extensive fields could rear countless monarchs that make the amazing migration to Mexico each year—another unanticipated legacy of the Bennetts. As the trail continues into Silver Creek and Terra Cotta Conservation Areas, you'll occasionally encounter small pockets of old-growth forest—though nothing to rival Scotsdale Farm—as well as small streams, waterfalls, and open-grown wolf trees (see the Humber Valley Heritage Trail, page 215, to learn more about wolf trees).

You may also wish to explore the Bruce Trail south of Trafalgar Road. Go back to the fork of the Bennett Trail but continue south on the Bruce Trail (it briefly follows Trafalgar Road to the east before crossing). This trail continues to follow the cedar–hemlock swamp southwest of Trafalgar Road, with scattered cedar trees or groves that reach 120-to 140-years-old. However, the nicest patch of old growth is a small grove of sugar maple, hemlock, and some basswood where the trees are 150-to 230-years-old (43.67446, -79.99105). This patch of old-growth forest, less than one kilometre down the trail from the junction, is actually contained within Scotsdale Farm at the southern end of the land the Bennetts owned.

Scotsdale Farm is part of the largest natural area in the Halton Region—40 square kilometres of wetlands, ravines, swamp, and upland forest that includes Silver Creek and Terra Cotta Conservation areas. It is important habitat for migratory birds, raptors, and many other animals, and it connects (with only a few significant interruptions) all the way to Crawford Lake and even Cootes Paradise.

Beaver Valley

✤ What you'll like

The Harshman Property in Beaver Valley offers a varied hike through shady forest and field along the Bruce Trail, with large old-growth sugar maple trees, and a beautiful descent down a stream valley with views of two small waterfalls. This tends to be a quiet section of the Bruce Trail and there are plenty of opportunities for longer hikes.

✤ How to get there

By car – The closest parking is on Graham's Hill Road, a little above the trail crossing. There's an obvious pullout with space for several cars (44.33361, -80.55496). Walk down the hill and turn left on the Bruce Trail.

By public transit – Buses run to Flesherton; check Grey Bruce Airbus (greybruceairbus.com) or Grey Transit Route (grey.ca/grey-transit-route) for routes and schedules. From Flesherton, a 3 km walk along country roads will get you to the Bruce Trail on East Back Line (44.28012, -80.54620). From there it is around 9 km on the trail to reach the old-growth forest north of Graham's Hill.

By bike – There are a number of cycle routes that pass close to Beaver Valley, mostly following country roads shared with cars. The CP Rail Trail runs from Orangeville to Owen Sound. However, the southern part of the trail is loose gravel that provides a poor surface for many bikes. Between Owen Sound and Holland Centre, the trail is packed stone dust that offers a reasonably good surface for most bikes. The CP Rail Trail passes within about 8 km of the trailhead, via Road 110 and Concession 12.

✤ What to do

On the whole, this is a very nice walk, which could be easily enjoyed in a round trip of two to three hours, though you'll be out of breath on the return

This cascading stream in the Beaver Valley is one of many hidden wonders along the Bruce Trail.

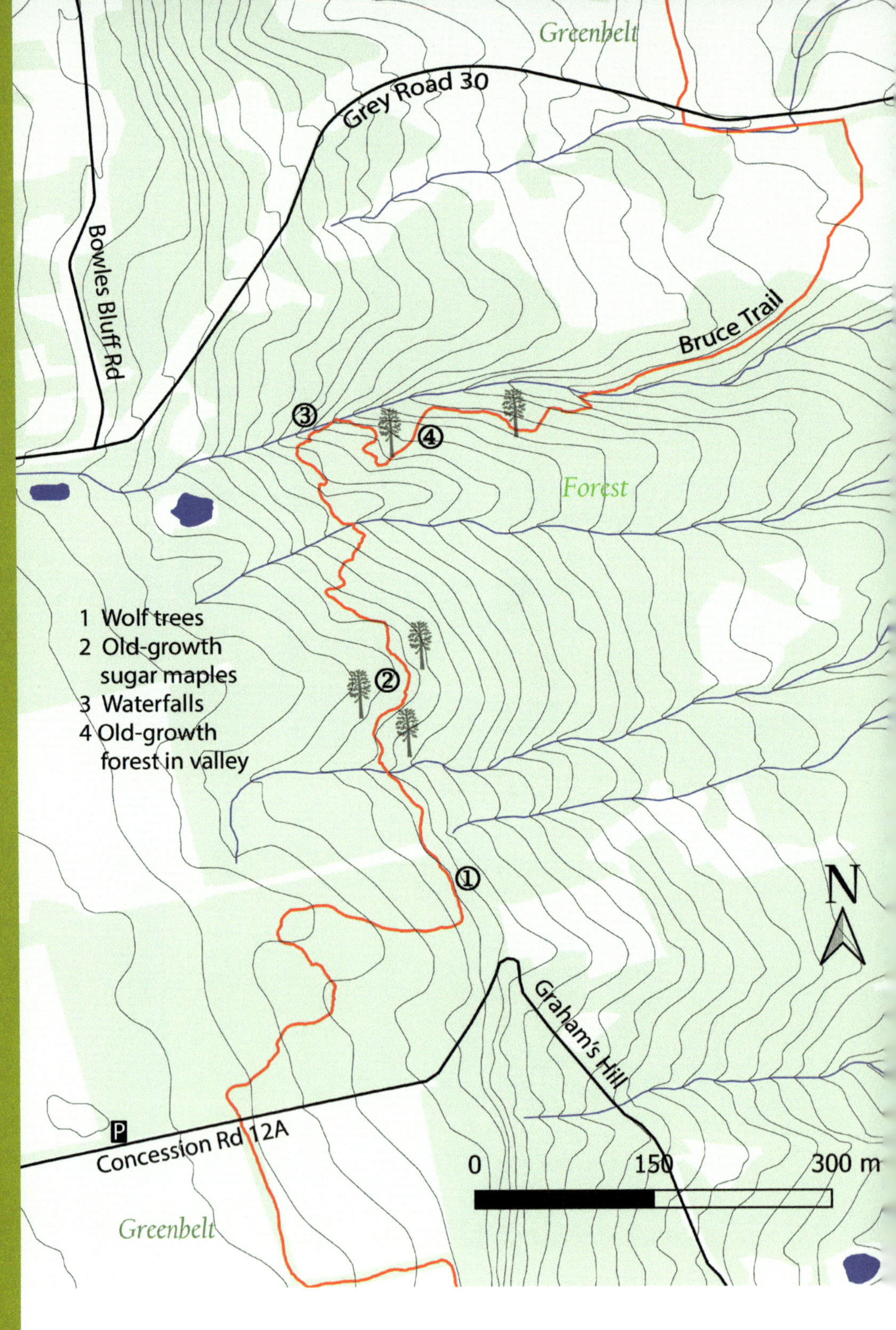

Greenbelt
Grey Road 30
Bowles Bluff Rd
Bruce Trail
③
④
Forest
1 Wolf trees
2 Old-growth
sugar maples
3 Waterfalls
4 Old-growth
forest in valley
②
①
N
Graham's Hill
P
Concession Rd 12A
0
150
300 m
Greenbelt

trip. While you're in the area, you can continue your hike on the Bruce Trail, and/or visit Eugenia Falls. Don't miss out on restaurants and cafés in Flesherton, and the Flying Chestnut restaurant in Eugenia, if it's open.

✣ Learn more

The Bruce Trail was opened in 1967, Canada's Centennial year, after seven years of effort. The idea of the trail was first brainstormed at a meeting of the Federation of Ontario Naturalists in 1960, and regional clubs for the trail were established in 1963. Parts of the Bruce Trail run through parks and conservation land or private nature reserves, many of which have been donated by landowners or purchased with donated funds. By 2020, over 11,000 acres of Escarpment land had been preserved by the Bruce Trail Conservancy. Roughly a third of the Bruce Trail still runs across private land with the agreement of the landowners.

A member of the Beaver Valley Club of the Bruce Trail Conservancy calculated that every fifth step on the Beaver Valley section of the Bruce Trail is on a private landowner's property. It's an amazing model, and I feel privileged to walk on this trail that was created by generosity—not just of landowners but also the many volunteers who reach out to landowners, who build and maintain the trail, and re-route it when things change. The Bruce is not a static trail but a living, shifting thing. In one year, the Beaver Valley chainsaw crew spent over 600 volunteer hours clearing fallen trees off the trail.

The Beaver Valley is significant for its large intact forest area, which provides habitat for 22 interior forest bird species and four raptor species. Because of this, dogs should be kept on leash, particularly in spring and early summer when they can disturb ground-nesting birds. Some sections of trail are off limits to dogs altogether. These may be on private land where owners' dogs or livestock feel threatened by strange dogs passing through. Whatever the reason, remember the accord between hikers, volunteers, and landowners that holds the Bruce Trail together, and follow the rules. Many landowners go above and beyond simply allowing the trail; to cross their land. One built a viewing platform along the trail, one used their ATV to haul equipment to a section of the trail for the maintenance crew, while another allowed a picnic area to be created on their land. They do this because they love the trail, and it's not rare for some landowners to donate their land to the trail conservancy, during their lifetimes or after their death.

The trail in this section of Beaver Valley crosses through a mix of private land and a property that was donated by the Harshman family to the Ontario Heritage Trust, which is where the most impressive old-growth forest is found. It's a nice 150+-year-old sugar maple forest, with some large trees. Just before you reach it there are some charming wolf (open-grown) trees along the old fence line. The patch of old growth is small, and barely a destination on its own, but continue along the trail and follow a stream down a lovely series of cascades with views of two waterfalls. All along this stream is relatively old hemlock and sugar maple forest, where trees are commonly 100 to 150-years-old. The stream and the surrounding forest make for a magical descent into the valley, and a lovely walk in a charming part of Ontario.

If you have the time, plan to make this part of a larger hike along the Bruce Trail. You may also want to visit Eugenia Falls, an impressive drop in a steep gorge. Though enough water is diverted for hydro power, it can be just a trickle in the drier months. I also need to put in a plug for The Flying Chestnut Kitchen (FCK), started by Chef Shawn Adler, and featuring Indigenous and local fare. I used to eat at his amazing restaurant in Peterborough, then in 2010 he opened the FCK in Eugenia on the site of what was once the old general store. Adler also ran the Pow Wow Café in Toronto's Kensington Market, and in 2022 became a television star as a celebrity chef judge on the Food Network's *Wall of Chefs*. Unfortunately, the Flying Chestnut is only open sporadically—you can check regular updates on their Facebook page or try calling them.

Old-growth forest on the Harshman property in the Beaver Valley.

The Horse Lake Trail in Bruce Peninsula National Park

✣ What you'll like

This is a good trail for views of Georgian Bay and to see the huge ecological range of eastern white cedar. Old cedars are found growing in swamp, on a rock face, and on rocky beaches. Get close enough to touch ancient cedars nestled in a small overhang, enjoy the clear blue-green waters of Georgian Bay, and continue as far as you like along the Bruce Trail.

✣ How to get there

By car – The Horse Lake Trail begins at the Cyprus Lake day use/camping area; parking at the end of Cyprus Lake Road can be reserved ahead.

By public transit – There is little in the way of transit to the Bruce Peninsula. You can check Parkbus, which may offer seasonal service, or some private tour operators might get you there.

By bike – There are a number of official Bruce County Cycling Routes on smaller roads to the south of Bruce Peninsula National Park. However, Hwy 6 offers relatively poor cycling.

✣ What to do

This hike combines nicely with a swim at the Grotto, a hike at Halfway Log Dump, or a boat trip to hike on Flowerpot Island. You can camp at Cyprus Lake Campground to get out ahead of the crowds in the morning. It can be busy here in peak season; you might want to come in the off season unless you're committed to swimming in cold water in the heat of summer.

✣ Learn more

My plan was to follow the Horse Lake Trail to the beach, then clamber along

Cedar trees over 150-years-old grow in the swamp along the Horse Lake Trail.

the rocks at the end looking for ancient cedars on the low escarpments found there. These small dwarf cedars can be many centuries old, often hanging from a crevice so small they might appear to be growing out of solid rock. To my surprise, I soon found myself walking on a boardwalk winding through a small pocket of old-growth cedar swamp. Large moss-covered cedars lean over the trail, and alongside the boardwalk they sometimes stand with their feet in the water like reluctant bathers considering a dip. A ring count from a fallen tree revealed that the cedars here are at least 150-years-old, and some may be over 200-years-old.

It seems hard to imagine two more different habitats for the same tree to grow in than swamp and cliff, but the explanation is simple: cedars are specialists in growing where other trees won't. And, though a cliff may seem to be the driest of habitats, there's always some moisture creeping through the crevices where a cedar's roots are confined, so they can still keep their feet wet.

1 Old-growth cedar swamp
2 Old cedars growing below overhang
3 The Grotto
4 Boulder Beach
Georgian Bay
Lake Huron
Bruce
Horse Lake Trail
Bruce Peninsula
National Park
Cyprus Lake Rd
Horse
Lake
Georgian Bay Trail
Marr
Lake
Bruce Trail
Marr Lake Trail
P
0
250
500 m
Cyprus
Lake

This swamp forest is a lovely place to hang out (at least, outside of mosquito season). There's even a bench. Once you've appreciated the mossy cedars, further rewards await as you continue on to the beach. However, anyone who says they enjoy long walks on the beach probably isn't thinking of Bruce Peninsula National Park. The wave-rounded bleached rocks are beautiful, no doubt, but each step on them is unsettled. Will the stone tip? Will your foot slip? Will your ankle twist? It's not particularly dangerous per se, but it's tedious and tiring for long stretches. Fortunately, the whole beach is only half a kilometre long. The Bruce Trail will try to call you back into the woods but, if you ignore it, you can continue less than 100 metres past and look for ancient cedars hanging off limestone ledges at the end of the beach.

There are cedars all along the Bruce Peninsula. The oldest are found on large cliffs, such as the 40-metre-high escarpment at Lion's Head, where trees reach over 1300-years-old. But getting a good view of the ancient cedars on the massive cliff face is very difficult, requiring long scrabbles over loose trail-less talus slopes, or rappelling down the cliff face from above. In Bruce Peninsula National Park, it's different; the Niagara Escarpment dips close to the water at many points. The low rock faces, swept by wind and waves, aren't home to as many extremely ancient cedars. But you can see small cedars that are commonly 100-to 300-years-old or more, still beautiful and noteworthy. And which is more impressive: a centuries-old tree that would fit in the passenger seat of your car, that you can practically touch, or a millennium-old tree, maybe not much larger, that you'll never actually see? There is no right answer to that question; both are impressive in their own way.

As you continue to the stone ledges at the east end of the beach, there are several charismatic cedars hanging out of a small cave, their trunks spiralling around themselves. They are probably quite old, and they are so low that you can touch the branch tips. The inventories of ancient cedars in the 1990s and early 2000s never looked at Bruce Peninsula National Park, so we may never know the age of these trees, but I'd be surprised if they were less than 300-years-old, and they could be more. This spiralling growth form was compared to a waterfall by ancient-cedar researcher Doug Larson.

You may now wish to backtrack and begin climbing the hill to follow the Bruce Trail heading east. On either side of the trail below the ridge there are forest-grown cedars that are likely old growth. They are smaller than the cedars by the boardwalk on the way in but could be at least as old. At this point you may have noticed that size doesn't mean much with cedars—for most trees, the size is more related to the site where they're growing than it is to the age of the tree, but with cedars this is taken to the extreme!

The Bruce Trail has its own special beauty, winding along the limestone ledges and between square-edged boulders. It's also a good aerobic workout climbing up and down the ridge. At the next white-stone beach there are large cedars along the back of the beach that are likely also pretty old. You can continue as long as you like along the Bruce Trail and, if you keep your eyes open, you may see other trees that rival the upside down waterfalls on the ledges of the first beach. This walk leads you past old cedars on a wide variety of habitats: stony beach, shady forest, rock escarpment, and swamp. It's a testament to the versatility of eastern white cedar trees. Consider that the most common species making up hedges in the suburbs is also the oldest tree in Ontario, living over 1300 years and hanging off a 40-metre cliff! Cedars like calcareous soils, but they can also grow on granite rock outcrops and are sometimes found in acidic bogs. They grow in old-growth forests and in abandoned fields. Ecologically, they're hard to peg down.

There's an old story that goes like this: when Jacques Cartier overwintered on the shores of Quebec in 1535–1536, his crew suffered

Many cedars in Bruce Peninsula National Park are centuries old but have never been studied.

from terrible scurvy (teeth falling out, etc.), but they were miraculously cured when the people of Stadacona brewed a tea made from the leaves of an evergreen tree called Aneda. For years we learned that this tree was the eastern white cedar, which was gifted the name "arborvitae" (tree of life) by the king of France, for its healing powers. Now we're not so sure; maybe it was balsam fir. Either way, next time you're suffering from scurvy, the cure is likely near at hand—you might want to boil some needles from your neighbour's hedge, or from your Christmas tree. Either way, boil up quite a bit; one Quebec historian estimates that 80 kg of foliage was boiled in a large copper pot (more of a cauldron) to cure Cartier's crew. But not too much,

as white cedar can be toxic in large quantities, and pregnant women should avoid drinking cedar tea since it was historically used to induce abortions.

What's less often mentioned in the upbeat story of the tree of life is that when Cartier returned to France in 1536, he kidnapped Donnacona, the chief of Stadacona, and brought him with him. Three years later, Donnacona died there.

On your drive home you'll pass many fields with split-rail fences made from cedar trees, a testament to the rot resistance of the tree. Which, I think, is more than mere coincidence—you can't be an easy meal for insects and micro-organisms if you're going to live for 1000 years.

Flowerpot Island (Fathom Five National Marine Park)

✣ What you'll like

Flowerpot Island is a gem, nestled in the clear aquamarine waters of Georgian Bay, with good views of ancient cedars growing on its shoreline. Also, of course, the famous flowerpot rock formations for which it is named, and shipwrecks seen from the glass-bottom boat on the ferry ride across. There's something for everyone there.

✣ How to get there

The only way to get to Flowerpot Island is by boat, a 6.5 km trip from Tobermory harbour. Two private tour boat companies operate return trips (every 1½ hours) from Tobermory to the island from mid May to mid October (weather permitting). www.blueheronco.com, www.bruceanchorcruises.com

By car – Tobermory can be reached in under four hours by car from the Greater Toronto Area.

By public transit – Parkbus operates buses to Tobermory (parkbus.ca), with pickup points in downtown Toronto or Brampton. It is roughly a five-and-a-half-hour trip.

By bike – Explore The Bruce has published maps of Bruce County Cycling Routes. Bicycles can be taken for free on the Chi-Cheemaun ferry to Manitoulin Island.

✣ What to do

Going to Flowerpot Island is already an event. The ferry to the island is typically a glass-bottom boat that tours shipwrecks along the way. Plan to bring food and lots of water, probably a swimsuit, and spend at least

One of the best places to see ancient cedars is at the south bluff. The cedar at top germinated in 1179, making it around 850-years-old.

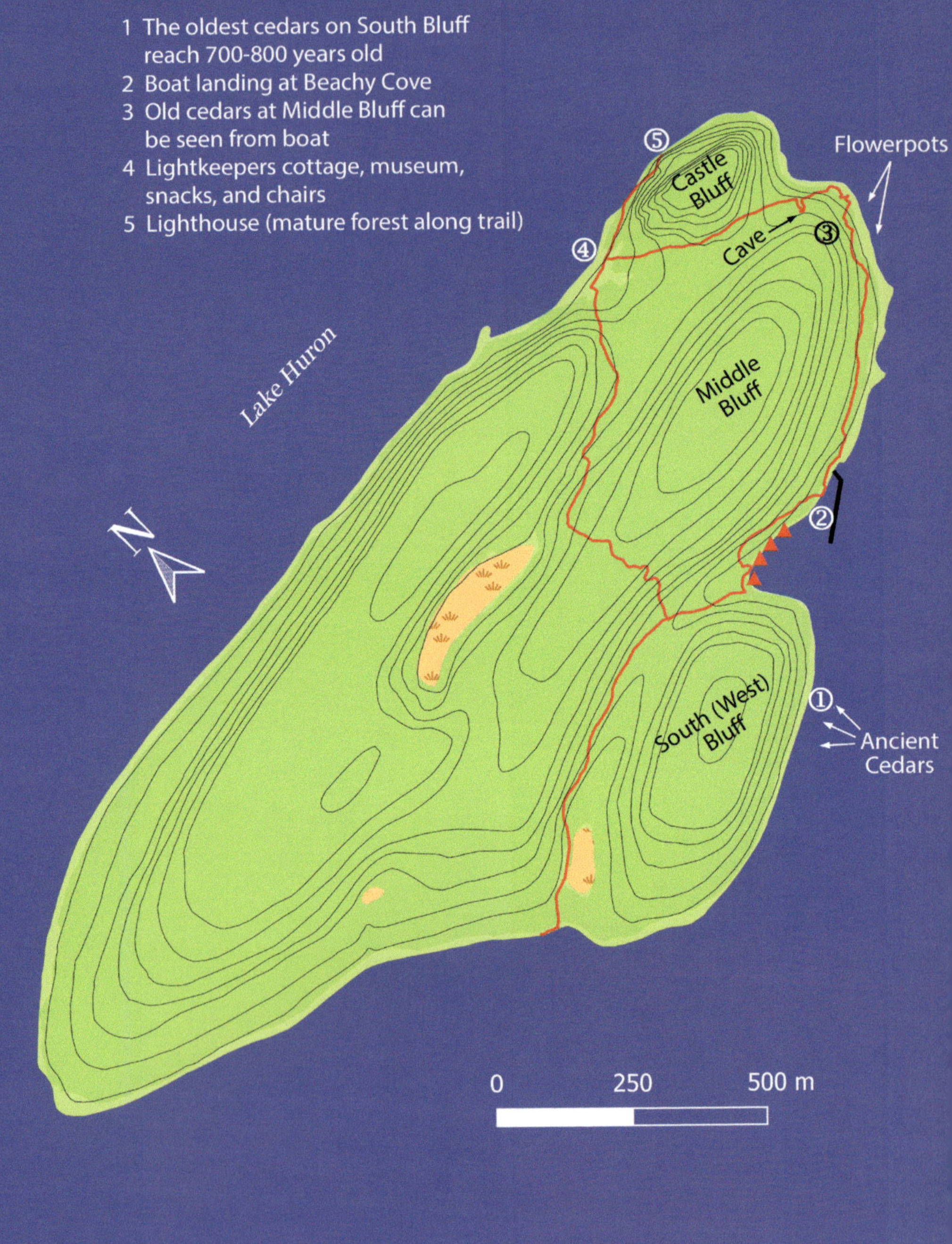
1 The oldest cedars on South Bluff reach 700-800 years old
2 Boat landing at Beachy Cove
3 Old cedars at Middle Bluff can be seen from boat
4 Lightkeepers cottage, museum, snacks, and chairs
5 Lighthouse (mature forest along trail)
Flowerpots
Castle Bluff
Cave
Lake Huron
Middle Bluff
N
South (West) Bluff
Ancient Cedars
0
250
500 m

three to four hours on the island. Swimming on the ledges around the flowerpots is very popular in hot weather if the waves aren't too big. If you want to really experience the island and are up for an adventure, consider camping there. It will be a completely different experience after the last boat leaves, taking the rest of the tourists with it, effectively stranding you in the quiet of the night beneath a few thousand stars (and probably some other campers nearby).

Learn more

After the accidental discovery of centuries-old ancient cedars near Milton in 1988 (read more in Rattlesnake Point and Crawford Lake pages), researchers from the University of Guelph worked their way up the escarpment over the next few years, rappelling down cliffs to seek out Ontario's oldest trees, and finding trees reaching up to an incredible 1032-years-old. That, however, was only the beginning.

In 1993 Pete Kelly was surveying a cliff on an island of Fathom Five National Marine Park, when he realized it might be worth looking more closely at the dead wood littering the talus at the base of the cliff. When he examined a cross-section from the weathered trunk of one dead cedar, he was able to count 1567 annual growth rings, and he estimated the age to be close to 1890 years! Another trunk revealed a continuous count of 1653 rings. In their book *The Last Stand*, Kelly and Larson describe the strangely deformed trunk of this tree as resembling a "bag of knotted ropes."

Another high point came when they reached Lion's Head in 2003, whose 40-metre cliffs are, in more ways than one, the most spectacular refuge of ancient cedars in Ontario. Here they found more than 50 trees over 500-years-old, an incredible 10 trees over 1,000-years-old, and the oldest living tree in Ontario, which germinated in the year 688 AD! There were actually two trees at Lion's head around 1300-years-old.

The ledges around the flowerpots are a popular place for swimming.

The trouble with Lion's Head is that it's hard for anyone who's not a skilled rock climber to see the ancient cedars. A few can be seen at the cliff base, but there are no trails over the leg-breaker talus slope, which ranks among the worst footing I've encountered. Contrast that with the low bluffs of Flowerpot Island, where as the ferry approaches (or leaves) the shore, you might get a view of a cedar that germinated in the year 1179 on the south bluff.

At first glance this cedar looks dead. However, it is only mostly dead—and as Billy Crystal reminds us in *The Princess Bride*, "There's a big difference between mostly dead and all dead. Mostly dead is slightly alive." No one knows this better than an ancient cedar. The tree on the south bluff (which Doug Larson has dubbed "the alien") was mostly *alive* until the year 1849. In that year for some reason (maybe there was a local drought, or the flow of water through cracks in the rock shifted), most of the tree died and a single low-hanging branch was all that remained alive

Ancient cedars on South Bluff.

on the tree. This kind of thing is common with ancient cedars, and that branch could go on to live for another millennium!

This habit of partially dying creates a number of characteristics that can be helpful in identifying ancient cedars. One key feature is a very asymmetrical trunk. The portion of the tree that is still alive continues to grow in one direction, making the trunk less and less round—at the extreme it can come to resemble the "bag of ropes" Kelly and Larson describe. Some trees may simply grow as a long oval or almost flat trunk, and still others may be a spiral. But basically, old trees are strange looking, often mostly dead, and sometimes hanging upside down. They're also often small—or certainly smaller than most forest trees—because root growth is limited, which in turn restricts growth of the crown.

And they're surrounded by a lot of rock. One of the tricks for staying alive for many centuries is to be isolated from dangers such as forest fire and browsing, so isolation is the starting point when looking for ancient cedars. At Flowerpot Island, ancient cedars can be seen from the boat tours that take you to the island, but you often need binoculars to get a good look at them. Many small cedars on the flowerpots, cliffs, and caves around the island are older than their size would suggest. A cedar hanging off the side of the small flowerpot is under a metre long and is of unknown age—it's hard to say if it measures its age in decades or centuries, but at least it's probably older than you are! Some very old cedars can be seen on the high cliffs that form a backdrop to the large flowerpot, including one that hangs upside down. You can make it out with the naked eye, but binoculars will let you get a good look at it and other ancient cedars on this cliff face (tour boats circle to give a view of the flowerpot—and, conveniently, the ancient cedars behind it).

As you hike the trails around Flowerpot Island, you're usually walking under a canopy of cedar trees. This cedar forest is often over 100-years-old, and in places over 150 years. The trail to the lighthouse has some old-growth cedars, which can be recognized by their large twisting limbs—though they're nowhere near as old as ancient cedars growing on the island's cliffs and bluffs. It's worth stopping to have a look at the lighthouse museum. Chips, candy, and cold drinks can be purchased at the concession in the museum and enjoyed in the rocking chairs arrayed on the porch.

Few cedars match the "alien" on south bluff for access and old age—but its not exactly easy to get to. To reach south bluff you can follow the rocky beach past campsite one (the old wharf at campsite two marks a good point to leave the loop hiking trail). Once you duck under a rocky overhang and reach a large boulder, you can start looking for ancient cedars, including the 850-year-old cedar with its one living branch snaking down the rock face. Many other stunted cedars on these low cliffs are very old, including four more trees over 700-years-old, and another

This gull is pretty sure Flowerpot Island belongs to it.

over 600 years. Depending on the water level, you may get wet feet at the overhang, but mostly it's a scramble over rocks and small boulders—so gauge whether that sounds like it's for you. Even though it's a short distance, you should allow one to two hours to get there and back and have a look at the cedars.

Greater Toronto River Valley and Headwaters

Bronte Creek

✤ What you'll like

Bronte Creek Park features a spectacular 50-metre-deep ravine, with dwarfed 240-year-old hemlocks on the steep slopes. Beside the ravine is an old-growth hardwood forest with impressive maple and beech trees that are as old as the hemlocks. A somewhat younger maple forest nearby boasts a spectacular spring show of trilliums. As a special treat, Bronte Creek is home to several disease-resistant beech trees, one of which is easily seen along the trail.

✤ How to get there

By car – The Park entrance is 1.6 kilometres north-west of Hwy 403 on Burloak Drive. The trails through old-growth forest can be accessed most easily from Parking Lot A or F.

By public transit – From Burlington, follow the Waterfront Trail and Centennial Bikeway to Burloak Dr; continue North to the park.

By bike – From Appleby GO station take Burlington Transit bus #11

Hemlocks on the steep valley slopes of Bronte Creek reach 240-years-old.

(Sutton–Alton). Get off at the first stop on Sutton Drive and walk 15 to 20 minutes to Bronte Creek Provincial Park.

✤ What to do

The park is particularly beautiful in the spring when the trilliums are blooming, or autumn when the colours are changing. Walk both the Ravine Trail and the Trillium Trail for sure, and the Half Moon Trail is also worthwhile. Plan to have lunch at the park's picnic areas, visit the Spruce Lane Farmhouse to learn more about the lifestyle of early farmers, as well as the Nature Centre and Children's Farm and Play Barn in summer. In winter there is cross-country skiing and a toboggan hill. An advantage of going in winter is you can see farther into the woods.

✤ Learn more

Bronte Creek is a good vantage point from which to consider colonization. Not from a beat-yourself-up perspective, nor a denial or shoulder-shrug perspective, but to actually trace moments in history and consider how we got here (literally and figuratively). This is because Bronte Creek was one of the last places on the north shore of Lake Ontario to be ceded by treaty and developed by European settlers (that is, one of the last places to be colonized). The treaty (Treaty 22, in 1820—more on that later) was between the British and the Mississauga Anishinaabeg Nation, which speaks to centuries of conflict leading up to that moment.

When French settlers first arrived on the continent, the Wendat (Huron) ostensibly controlled the area, though most of their permanent settlements were further north beyond the reach of Haudenosaunee (Iroquois) raiding parties. The Anishinaabeg (Ojibwe) also often had treaties to share resources with the Wendat, and might have been found fishing seasonally at the river mouths. By the mid 1600s the Haudenosaunee were conquering

1 150-year-old maple-oak forest in ravine
2 240-year-old dwarf hemlocks on steep slopes
3 240-year-old maple and beech forest.
4 Disease resistant beech trees
Bronte Creek
Ravine Trail
Logging Trail
Trillium Trail
Bronte Creek Provincial Park
Bronte Rd
Hwy 403
N
P
0.5
1 km

many neighbouring territories to gain access to pelts for the fur trade. In 1649 they ultimately defeated the Wendat, and many of the survivors fled to Quebec or Detroit, or joined with other Indigenous Nations.

For a while the Haudenosaunee controlled the north shore of Lake Ontario, and they continued to expand and clash with other Indigenous Nations. Most consequential was a growing enmity and increasing number of skirmishes between the Haudenosaunee and the Anishinaabeg neighbouring nation to the north, who had once been allied with the Wendat and had welcomed some of their refugees. Ultimately an Anishinaabeg coalition would defeat the Haudenosaunee in a series of battles culminating at the end of the 17th century. History, of course, is messy and, depending on who is telling it (the Haudenosaunee, the Anishinaabeg, or the British), some of that history would probably be told differently. I do my best; it still needs to be told.

But however we look back on it (and probably as understood at the time), it was a bitter victory—the fur trade and associated alliances with Europeans had fuelled the wars that ultimately, combined with introduced diseases and destruction of the environment and resources they depended on, weakened all the Indigenous Nations involved. This was the blunt cudgel of colonization, though, as we know, it didn't stop there. What followed is what is usually referred to as "settler colonization," which is codified in laws and political structures and required treaties to lend it a veneer of legitimacy.

When the treaties were being negotiated, the Mississaugas of the Credit First Nation held a large tract of what is now among the most valuable land in Canada, part of the "Golden Horseshoe" of southern Ontario. What probably happened next was that they sat down (most likely outdoors) with representatives of the Crown, and a great deal was said, many promises were made, only a small fraction of which were written

This fallen beech tree still shows the carved love declarations that often mark the species. Until recently, the trees nearly always outlasted the lovers, but lately the odds have changed.

down in the treaty. The oral agreements made that day were quickly forgotten by the British, but not by the Mississauga Anishinaabeg who have an oral tradition of knowledge keeping. The larger problem, though, might have been the basic understanding of land ownership. This would have been a foreign concept to Indigenous peoples, and treaties between Indigenous Nations would have always been understood as agreements on how to share land and resources. Though I said earlier that the land was ceded by treaty, this is probably inaccurate from the perspective of Indigenous peoples, who would have considered the land as shared, and always sought to maintain hunting and fishing rights.

Bronte Creek was one of three river valleys that were still held by the Mississauga Anishinaabeg in 1820, and they must have kept it at least partly for the abundant fish resources that it held. Looking at the broad riffles of the river today, it's easy to imagine the native (lake-bound) Atlantic salmon teaming in the river, running so thick, the story goes, they could be scooped out with a shovel—though, typically, the salmon were speared by Indigenous people, and later netted by European settlers. American eels and other native fish were also abundant.

After 1820, European settlers quickly established their own salmon fisheries at Bronte Creek. However, they also built many dams on the river to power sawmills and gristmills, which, combined with overfishing and deforestation, led to the collapse of the salmon fisheries. The Bronte Creek watershed was once a heavily forested landscape, but by the 1920s it had less than 10% forest cover, and the resulting warmer water would make it harder for salmon to survive and reproduce. At least one family, however, maintained a small woodlot of maple, oak and beech forest that was never completely cleared. And the steep ravine slopes along the creek were clothed in dense hemlock forest. The larger hemlock trees were probably cut from the ravine slopes (an impressive feat) and used to build barns or frame homes. But the smaller hemlocks were left, and many of them remain to this day.

Today these forests are all protected in Bronte Creek Provincial Park. In both the small woodlot and the adjacent ravine slopes, the oldest trees reach about 240-years-old, predating settlement of the area by about 40 years. A walk along the Ravine Trail is ideal to see both types of old-growth forest. On one side are dwarfed hemlock trees on a steep slope. While they are less than half the size of the trees on the rich soils above, they are often as old or older than the large, impressive trees towering over them. The hemlocks show their age in flattened, slow-growing tops and relatively thick, twisting branches; they take on a bonsai look.

In the woodlot above are impressive big old maple and oak, and occasional beech trees. This forest can be seen from the Ravine Trail and on the north side of the Logging Trail (the south side was, as the name suggests, logged). Look for thick twisting branches high on the tree, and bark balding at the base, as indicators of old age on the maple trees. Once beech was a common tree here, but only a few remain.

The smooth grey bark of the beech tree makes it one of Ontario's most charismatic and easily identified trees (the trunks resemble elephant legs, which inspired the mnemonic "elephants walking on the beach" that I learned as a student). Many of Bronte Creek's old-growth beech trees have died in the last decade, victims of an invasive scale insect, which when combined with a fungus causes beech bark disease.

Beech trees are quickly killed by beech bark disease, while a few linger on with diseased bark and deformed trunks. There are, however, a small number of beech trees that remain healthy and unmarked while the trees around them succumb to the disease. These are resistant trees, that have natural defenses against the beech scale. Only between one and five percent of beech trees have resistance, but it can be passed on to their progeny,

The striking smooth grey bark of a disease-resistant beech tree.

so these trees are very important to the future of the species. There are several disease-resistant beech trees in the Bronte Creek forest, including one that is easily seen north of the logging trail. Finding a disease-resistant beech tree is a thrill, and for me it always brings a surge of hope. Yes, this beautiful tree that I knew from my youth is disappearing, but not entirely. And I can actually *do something* to restore it by helping to locate individual trees that seed collectors and researchers need to accelerate the recovery of the species. Resistant beech trees can be reported with the iNaturalist app (www.inaturalist.org/projects/beech-bark-disease-resistance).

Just as Bronte Creek is one of the places that holds the key to the restoration of American Beech, it is part of the reintroduction of Atlantic salmon to Lake Ontario. The last time a native Atlantic salmon was caught in Lake Ontario was in 1898—since then, this once abundant fish has been considered locally extinct. The salmon you see jumping at the Humber River and other Lake Ontario tributaries are unrelated Pacific salmon species that were introduced in the 1960s—but Atlantic salmon may again be seen swimming up Ontario's rivers to spawn. Since 2006, the Lake Ontario Atlantic Salmon Restoration Program has been releasing the fish into Lake Ontario tributaries, including Duffins Creek and Bronte Creek.

The head of the Toronto Carrying Place

✣ What you'll like

Walk the remnants of the thousands-of-years-old Toronto Carrying Place trail, past historic neighbourhoods and views of the Humber River, and watch seasonal salmon runs. Scattered along the route are very old and charismatic oak trees. They are now street trees but some of them once lined the carrying place trail. Don't miss the opportunity for a meal or a drink in Bloor West Village.

✣ How to get there

By car – Street parking is available in many places along the Carrying Place route.

By public transit – The Carrying Place route runs right past the Jane Street subway station, which makes a fine starting point for a 1 to 4 hour walk.

By bike – Coming from the east or west near the lakeshore, the Martin Goodman/Waterfront trail provides excellent access to Riverside Drive with only a few hundred metres along the Kingsway. From the north you can pick up the Humber River Recreational Trail. There are also several Bike Share locations in the area.

✣ What to do

This could be a short walk along Riverside Drive and a lunch at one of the great pubs or restaurants in Bloor West Village; or a more ambitious multi-hour walk through neighbourhoods and parks. A nice loop starts at the Jane Street subway and follows the Carrying Place through residential neighbourhoods via Rivercrest and Humbercrest. Cross Dundas Street at Howland, make your way into Lambton Park, and explore the ridge on established dirt trails. Follow a trail near the south of the park, which

A huge white oak near Riverside Drive may have once grown alongside the Toronto Carrying Place trail.

St Clair Ave W
Dundas St W
Humbercrest Blvd
Carrying Place Route (approximate)
Jane St
Baby Point
Humberview Rd
Rivercrest Rd
Riverside Dr
South Kings
Humber
P
1 Head of the trail, Rousseau House
2 Bloor West Village
3 Old Mill (subway, bike share, hotel)
4 Teiaiagon (Haudenosaunee Village)
5 Magwood Park (old-growth forest)
6 Lambton Park old-growth savannah
0 250 500 m

angles below the ridge to the multi-use trail along the river, and visit Lambton Woods and Magwood Park. Follow the River back to Old Mill Road and head back to Jane and Bloor. After lunch in Bloor West Village, walk down Riverside Drive to the start of the Carrying Place. Or reverse the itinerary and do the short walk down Riverside first. You might also consider bringing a bike and locking it while you explore Lambton Park. Bike Share is available at Jane subway, Étienne Brûlé Park, Old Mill, and near the bottom of the Kingsway/Humber Bay. There's a lot of potential for walk/bike combinations. Consider visiting High Park while in the area!

✤ Learn more

Toronto has its share of urban myths—take your pick. I like the alien base built in tunnels under Cabbagetown, or (more plausibly?) another UFO base under the waters of Lake Ontario. These stories raise some obvious questions, like "why so many bases?" and "are they from the same planet, or do they herald from entirely different worlds?" But we'll leave those questions for another, less factual book. The most enduring, pervasive, and best-pedigreed urban myth about the city was instigated by historian Henry Scadding in 1873. Scadding believed that the name Toronto derived from a Wendat (Huron) word "toi'onton" or "toronton," meaning "much" or "plenty." Somehow this was translated into "a place of meeting" or, as is commonly told today, "the meeting place."

It's a nice story, and it has stuck around because it's so appropriate for a city that was, in 2016, informally crowned by the BBC as the most multicultural in the world—with 51% of residents born outside of Canada, and 230 different nationalities living here. Unfortunately, it's probably not true. Toronto is certainly a meeting place, but it's not *the meeting place*. The actual derivation of Toronto is something along the lines of "trees standing in water," from the Mohawk word "tkaronto," referring to ancient fish

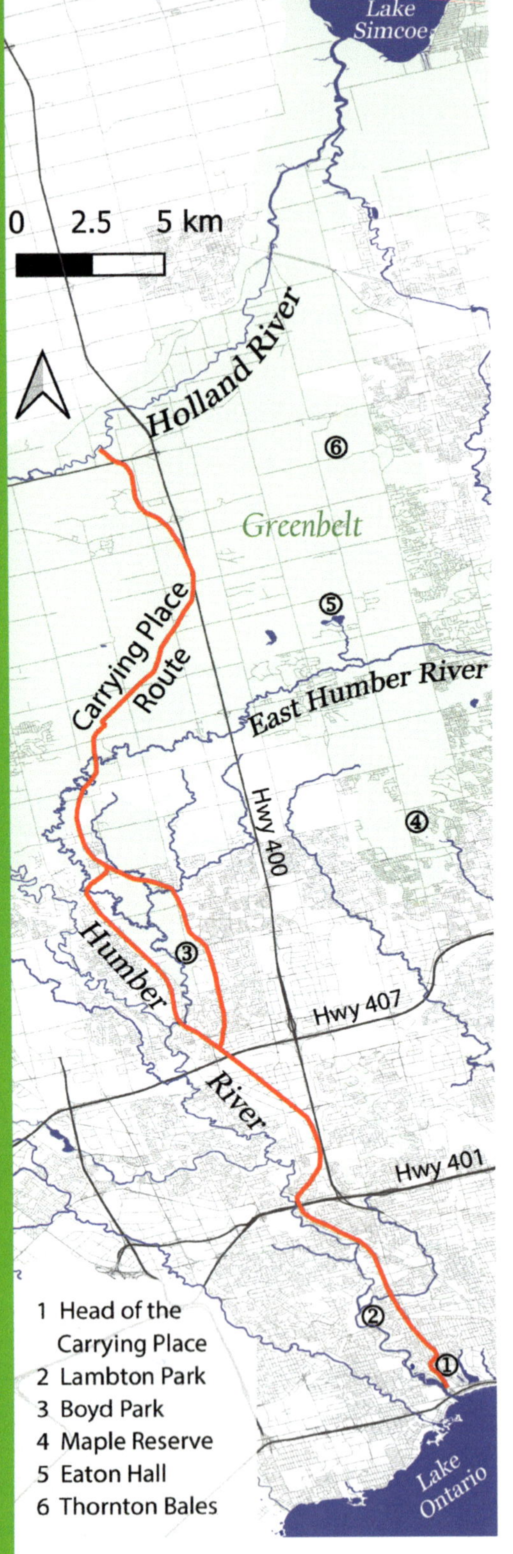

weirs in the Lake Simcoe–Couchiching narrows—essentially a bunch of poles driven into the lakebed, used to corral fish so they could easily be caught.

How did the city of Toronto come to be named for fish weirs in Lake Simcoe? To understand that we need to follow the course of the Toronto carrying place, an important historic trail with one end at the mouth of the Humber River and the other at the Holland River. From there it was only a short paddle into Lake Simcoe, historically known as Lake Taronto or Ouentironk ("Beautiful Water"). The fish weirs in the narrows of the lake were built over 5000 years ago and were incredibly productive, so much so that the area was considered sacred, and was used for many generations by the Wendat and Anishinaabeg people. It is now Mnjikaning Fish Weirs National Historic Site.

The Toronto trail may be equally ancient; it was certainly an important route linking Lake Ontario to Georgian Bay, via Lake Simcoe. Important enough that the Toronto Carrying Place was marked on many maps of the era, and it even appeared on a five-metre-diameter bronze globe that was commissioned by King Louis XIV. It was only one of many carrying places that connected different watersheds at the time—but an important one, and from the perspective of the modern city of Toronto, certainly the most important.

The name Toronto migrated south, first from the lake to the trail, and finally landing at roughly its current location when the French built Fort Toronto at the base of the carrying place, by the mouth of the Humber River, around the year 1750. The name was finally officially applied to the young, rapidly growing city in 1834, replacing the more mundane name of York. Would Toronto have been founded where it is today without the existence of the Carrying Place? Perhaps. There was a nice, sheltered harbour at the mouth of the Don River. Even if it had, it would probably still be called York, and would have lost out on some colourful stories.

All of this was on my mind as I began walking the famous millennia-old trail on one of those autumn days when the cold wind is more powerful than the watery sun. Specifically, I was walking on Riverside Drive, an asphalt road much like any other, except that it tends to wind as it follows a ridgetop—the same ridge the famous trail once followed. By the 1920s a housing development was built here, so the only remnants of the trail are oaks that once grew alongside it, now found in front yards of Riverside Drive. Some of these oaks reach 200-to 300-years-old, and collectively, the old oaks that mark the route of the carrying place trail have been named the Tuhbenahneequay Ancient Grove.

The location of the trees is always a bit vague when you hear about the grove, probably because they are mostly growing in people's yards. But at the height of land on Riverside Drive, there are some obviously rather old oak trees. Lucy Maud Montgomery, creator of *Anne of Green Gables*, had a house here later in life and there is a park named after her. The black oak trees in the park aren't especially old but there are two picnic tables and it's a nice place to sit and admire much older black oaks in the surrounding yards, as well as charming houses that have the look of English country homes. In addition to tall black oaks, there's a huge wide-spreading white oak at the corner of Riverside Trail that is a real landmark. Heading north on Riverside the oaks taper out, and you can cut right on Mossom Road to get to Bloor West Village, a posh but interesting neighbourhood.

You're following in the footsteps of thousands of First Nations people, some French explorers, and most recently Glenn Turner, who attempted to retrace the route of the trail and wrote the informative and entertaining book *The Toronto Carrying Place* in 2015. You may want to follow his footsteps all the way to the Black Horse Pub and keep him company for a pint before you pick up the route again at Rivercrest. If you read his book, you'll see that Turner called this section the Foot of the Carrying Place, which makes sense, but just doesn't have the same ring to it as the Head. You can call it whichever you like.

There are more large oaks along Rivercrest, and a few on Humbercrest, which also roughly parallels the ancient carrying place route. A short detour to the dead end of Langmuir Gardens takes you to a view through black oaks over mature hardwood forest on the slope. It's worth stopping here for a moment to imagine explorer and trader Étienne Brûlé pausing here for a drink of water, Wendat or Anishinaabeg families travelling south to fish salmon at the mouth of the Humber, or Mohawk raiding parties heading north. For a moment you can look out on a landscape of the distant past, before the founding of Toronto. I found myself suddenly humbled by the changes we've wrought over only a few human lifetimes, and wondering what comes next.

Incidentally, though the Carrying Place is sometimes called a portage, it is 45 kilometres long and almost no one carried their canoes. Instead, they

Oaks overhang Riverside Crescent, which can be reached by a set of stairs from Lucy Maud Montgomery Park.

walked for two days and then built new canoes at the far end of the portage, which it's said took only another two days. The only person known for certain to have carried canoes the length of the trail was French explorer LaSalle, in August 1681. It took him three weeks to make the trip.

Lambton Park and Lambton Woods

✣ What you'll like

Native prairie grasses and other unusual plants are found under scattered old-growth oaks and red pines in this ecologically rich and beautiful savannah in Toronto's west end. This is one of very few places in southern Ontario where red pine is found growing in a savannah forest. If you cross the river on a footbridge to Lambton Woods, you'll find yourself in a mature hardwood and hemlock forest.

✣ How to get there

By car – Parking is available in Lambton Park beside the arena. A playground can also be found there. Street parking is available in many places along the carrying place route.

By public transit – The #30 and #79 TTC buses stop nearby.

By bike – The Humber River Recreational Trail comes very close to the park. Coming from the east or west along the lakeshore, the Martin Goodman/Waterfront trail provides excellent access to Riverside Drive with only a few hundred metres along the Kingsway, and from there you can follow the Carrying Place route or pick up the Humber River Trail.

✣ What to do

You can combine Lambton Park with the Head of the Carrying Place Trail, as described in the previous section. Or it is a fine destination on its own, especially in late summer when wildflowers are blooming or in the autumn when the grasses are going to seed. Putter around in the prairie looking at plants and trees, or continue on to Lambton Woods—you can't go wrong. Bloor West Village remains a fine place to grab a drink or a meal.

Native flowers and grasses grow under red pine and black oak in this rare type of savannah.

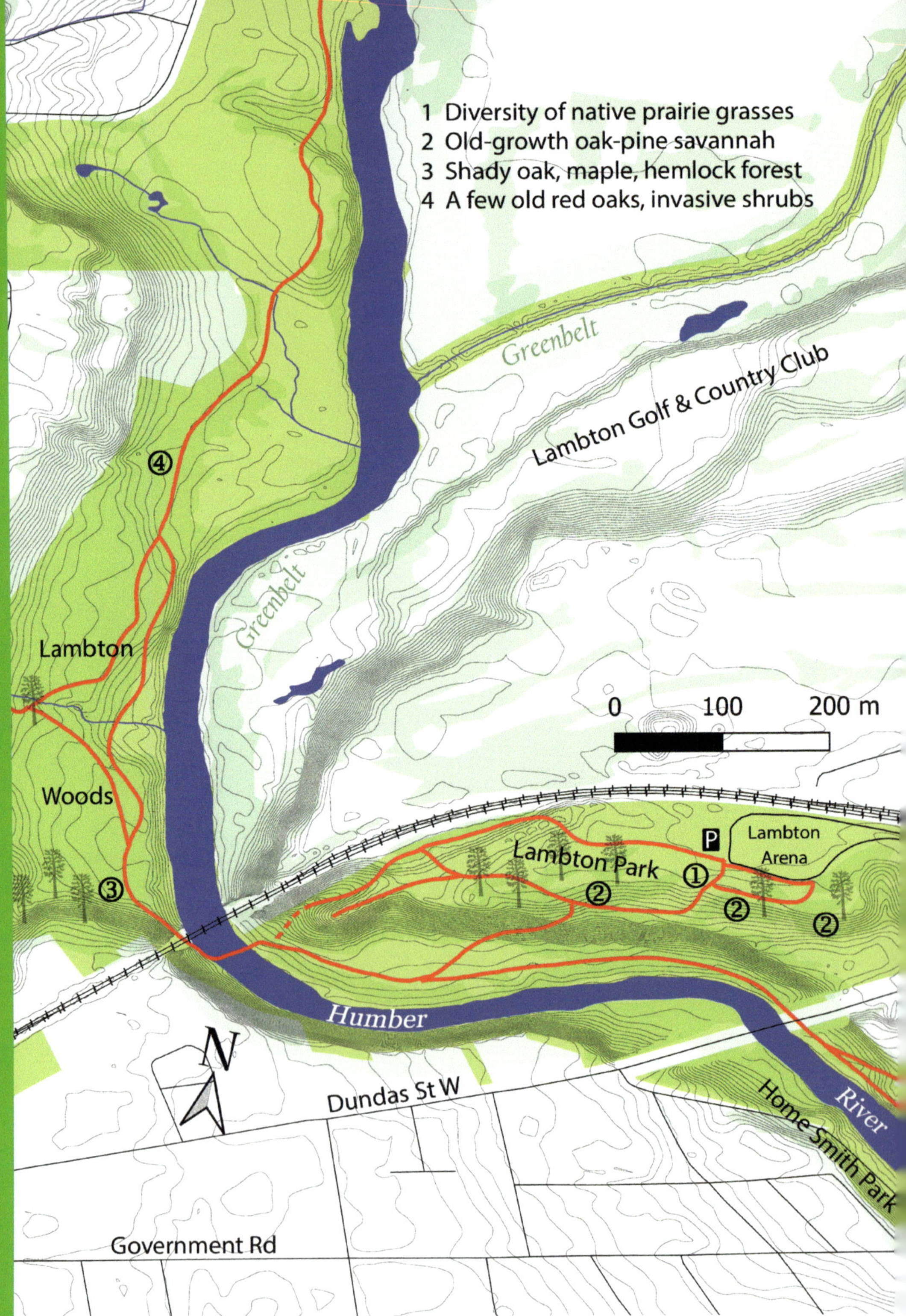
1 Diversity of native prairie grasses
2 Old-growth oak-pine savannah
3 Shady oak, maple, hemlock forest
4 A few old red oaks, invasive shrubs
Greenbelt
Lambton Golf & Country Club
Greenbelt
Lambton
Woods
0
100
200 m
P
Lambton Arena
Lambton Park
Humber
River
N
Dundas St W
Home Smith Park
Government Rd

✤ Learn more

This small but very important remnant of tallgrass savannah was once connected to similar oak savannah at High Park, but has long been cut off by urbanization. Nature nerds will be astonished to see old-growth black and white oak trees growing, mixed with red pine trees that sprouted after a fire more than 200 years ago. Red pine is a familiar tree to canoeists in northern forests of Temagami or the French River, but in southern Ontario is extremely rare outside of plantations. Within the Toronto Region, natural red pine is only found in Lambton Park, and a few individual trees in High Park.

Red pine's presence on the dry sandy ridge of Lambton Park tells us there was a long history of fire here. The seeds of red pine are small and adapted to grow on mineral soil exposed after a fire burns through—the bark of the tree is made of distinctive puzzle pieces that collectively create a fire-resistant surface. Fires that burn along the ground are rarely hot enough to kill the living inner bark. In fact, you may see charcoal at the base of some trees—evidence of one of the prescribed burns the city has undertaken to restore the ecological health of both Lambton and High Parks. Red pine is a very long-lived tree, capable of living for 500 years, so relatively hot fires might have happened only every century and still be enough to maintain red pine's presence here. But the prescribed burns the city has done haven't resulted in many young red pines, although there are quite a few oak and white pine seedlings. Either the red pines need the fire a little hotter, or maybe the burn just wasn't timed to a good seed year for them.

Black oak is one of the most common trees in Lambton Park. This tree has a few tricks of its own. For one, it is extremely tolerant of drought. Black oak seedlings can be killed by drought and grow back from the root system, so that the roots of black oak saplings may be 20 years older than

Little bluestem is a native prairie grass considered to be one of the best grasses for providing nesting and roosting habitat for birds, and it has very nutritious seeds.

the tops, having died back and resprouted one or several times. Likewise, if a black oak is killed by fire, it can resprout from the roots. Additionally, the bark at the base of the tree is moderately fire resistant.

Growing between the widely spaced trees is tallgrass prairie, and this, too, is maintained by fires that kill back competing shrubs. Indian grass, little bluestem and big bluestem are native prairie grasses growing just south of the arena parking area. Their distinctive flower and seed heads gain prominence in late summer and fall. The park is home to many significant plant species, including five that, within the Toronto region, are only found here and at High Park. Also hiding within the tall grasses, hunting insects and spiders, is the regionally rare smooth green snake, which is very sensitive to urbanization.

The biggest threats to Lambton Park are invasive species, off-leash dog walking, mountain biking, and its small size. Nearly a quarter of the species historically recorded in the area have disappeared over the past 120 years. The black oaks scattered through the neighbourhoods to the south-east bear testament to how extensive the savannah found in this park once was. If all the homeowners began planting native prairie grasses beneath the oaks, it would be a good start to restoring the savannah. It would also be beautiful.

As I left the park, I reflected on what I'd seen so far. The old oaks and the expansive history of the carrying place route captured my imagination in a way that few places in southern Ontario have done—but it was the shapely, diminutive, centuries-old red pines of Lambton Park that really floored me.

Lambton Woods is an entirely separate forest across the river, but it is only a 15-minute walk. To get there from Lambton Park, look for a trail near the south of the park cutting across the ridge and down into the valley to meet up with a paved multi-use trail. Like all the trails in Lambton Park, it's an informal dirt track; it's pretty easy to find when you're in the park but harder to spot from the paved trail, so take note of its location if you plan to find your way back. Head upriver and the multi-use trail soon crosses a pedestrian bridge over the Humber. On the other side, you enter into Lambton Woods.

This is a completely different forest type than the dry oak forest on the ridges, dominated instead by hemlock on the shady north-facing slope, and sugar maple on the flats, with scattered white pine and red oaks. The average tree is only 100-to 140-years-old, but there are a few scattered veterans that are well over 150-years-old. This is a forest that was historically logged and is just becoming old growth again. One of the biggest threats to it is invasive species. Invasive tree and shrub species are growing under the canopy, including Norway maple and European buckthorn. Most of the ash trees have been killed by the invasive emerald ash borer, while the hemlocks should be watched for the arrival of hemlock woolly adelgid.

Downstream from Lambton Park, the trail leads to Magwood Park, where there is a forest of similar age to Lambton Woods but less well known. There are mature sugar maples and red oaks, particularly on the slopes. There is also a decrepit stairway leading up to Baby Point. Interestingly, Baby Point (pronounced Babb-ee) was the site of the five nations Haudenosaunee village of Teiaiagon.

In September and October, you may see salmon leaping at any of the several low dams in Magwood and Étienne Brûlé Parks. Because the salmon have to jump there, the dam near Old Mill Road is considered the best place in Toronto to watch the salmon run. Atlantic salmon were abundant in Lake Ontario for millennia until they were wiped out in the 1800s, and today most of the salmon are western species that have been stocked for sport fishing. This may change because the Humber River is one of the sites where Atlantic salmon have been restocked.

Big bluestem grows under a canopy of red pine in Lambton Park.

The Rosedale Ravines

✤ What you'll like

The eco-industrial aesthetic of the Evergreen Brick Works makes a good starting point to explore these urban ravines, where several species of oak reach 150-to-200-years-old. The combination of beauty and accessibility makes Park Drive Ravine a rare gem in the heart of Toronto, and it can be combined with Moore Park Ravine or old Rosedale neighbourhoods of heritage homes, to form several possible loop routes. Parts of this ravine walk are only minutes away from a subway station!

✤ How to get there

By car – Evergreen Brick Works can be reached easily from the Don Valley Parkway. Exit at Bayview, follow Bayview north, and the entrance to the Brick Works will be almost immediately on your left (there is a turning lane, helpful when traffic volumes are high). At the time of writing, there are a few relatively slow EV chargers.

By public transit – Many transit access points are possible. From Summerhill subway station, a five-minute walk down Shaftesbury Ave leads to a stairway into the ravines. The Avoca Ave trail access is five minutes from St Clair subway station. And Craigleigh Gardens is a ten minute walk from Castle Frank subway. The #28 bus from Davisville Station stops at Evergreen Brick Works.

By bike – The Beltline Trail and Park Drive Reserve Trail run through the Rosedale Ravines. The Bayview Trail, Lower Don Trail, and Yonge Street Trail run nearby and provide access. There are also half a dozen Bike Share locations near the Rosedale Ravines, including at Evergreen Brick Works, Moore Park, and Avoca Avenue. Make sure to check for availability of bikes while planning your day.

The Evergreen Brick Works make a good starting point to explore the surrounding ravines.

✤ What to do

Consider going when the leaves are mostly off the trees for better views into the forest. Early spring at the start of leaf out can be beautiful if the trails are not too muddy. Autumn is also beautiful. Many routes are possible; here are two favourites.

On foot, walk from the Evergreen Centre along the edge of Bayview Avenue and into Park Drive Ravine. When you come to the fork, follow Milkman's Lane to the left and visit Craigleigh Gardens Park and possibly Beaumont Road, before following residential streets to Mathersfield Drive, where you can pick up trails to David A. Balfour Park (Rosehill Reservoir). Use one of the bridges below the park to cross Yellow Creek, and return on the broad multi-use Park Drive Reservation Trail. This loop can be started near Rosehill Reservoir if you're travelling by subway.

If you're on bicycle, you can make a loop up Park Drive Reservation Ravine (with an optional side trip up Milkman's Lane), through historic Mount Pleasant Cemetery, and back down Moore Park Ravine.

✤ Learn more

On a cool autumn day with the low sun angling through the trees, I walked in the Park Drive Ravine with Eric Davies, an ecologist who has taken Toronto's ravines under his wing. The Park Drive Ravine is important not only for its location, just off Yonge and Bloor in the heart of Toronto, but also because it offers, almost by accident, one of the best baseline studies showing 40 years of change in the Toronto ravines. In 2015 Davies went to a planning meeting for the ravines and met Paul Scrivener and Dale Taylor, two naturalists who had surveyed the ravines in 1977. Davies helped organize a group at the University of Toronto to resurvey the ravines and found that invasive Norway maple trees had jumped from 10% of forest cover to 40% over the past 40 years.

ount Pleasant
Mount Pleasant Rd
Cemetery
Bayview Ave
Moore Ave
St Clair Ave E
Inglewood Dr
Summerhill Ave
Bayview
Ave
borough St E
Beaumont Rd
Glen Rd
Don
River
Bloor St E
Rosedale Valley Rd
1 Evergreen Brickworks
2 Old oaks on slopes
3 Milkman's Lane
4 Craigleigh Gardens
5 Park Drive Ravine
6 Old Growth along rough trails
7 Avoca Avenue
8 Moore Park Ravine
N
0.5
1 km

A little grey is creeping into Davies's curly dark hair, revealing his middle age, but he moves through the world with the energy and enthusiasm of a 20-year-old, and a lot of it is aimed at trees. "I think Toronto has more forest than any large city in the world," he says. "Ravines are 17% of the city. If you walk across the city, one in five footsteps would land in a ravine." But, he says, we haven't been taking good care of them, despite special ravine legislation.

In addition to invasive trees, the understory of the ravines is also suffering; Davies feels it is "teetering on the brink." Native species are disappearing, replaced by invasive species. Some are seeding in from surrounding yards, or carried in with brush that is dumped into the natural areas. Others are aggressive invasives that are spreading everywhere, things like dog-strangling vine, garlic mustard, and Japanese knotweed. But Davies isn't pessimistic about the potential to reverse the trends. "It's like an old house–you can restore it. We have the technology," he says. All that has been lacking, at least up to this point, is the will to treat our ravines like a valuable asset. Attempts to put dollar values on trees have resulted in a range of results, but all agree on one thing: trees are worth a lot of money. "They're starting to assess the replacement value of trees. These trees are worth a hundred thousand dollars each," says Davies, and "we're putting graffiti on them, planting invasive species beside them."

He stops frequently to lift his binoculars, often to point out a bird, sometimes a crop of acorns or maple keys growing in a tree. "This has been a very good seed year for a lot of trees," he says. It's not a casual observation. Davies has over a thousand oak seedlings growing in his front yard, and he has distributed seeds to conservation authorities, municipalities, and other groups. Restoration of the ravines begins with planting truly local native trees that are adapted to grow there, and that starts with harvesting seed from Toronto's original trees.

The Rosedale ravines represent one of the most public faces of Toronto's

Eric Davies showing us oak seedlings that will be used to restore Toronto's ravines.

ravine system, in the heart of downtown and adjacent to the Evergreen Brick Works. This urban environmental education centre is built on the site of the Don Valley Brick Works, which operated from 1889 to 1984, making high quality fired-clay bricks that were used in the construction of many of Toronto's buildings, including Casa Loma, Massey Hall, and U of T's Hart House, to name a few. As I write this, I'm sitting in an office in Peterborough's historic Commerce Building, which was built with bricks from the Don Valley (the building is now an incubator for Peterborough artists and the heart of the First Friday art crawl). As early as 1926, the exposed soils of the Brick Works quarry revealed layers that geologists used to help reconstruct earth's history and changing climate. Beginning in 2006, the site was used to host a farmer's market, and soon after, the environment centre was built. As well as educational programs, you can stop for coffee or a meal.

The crown of this white oak shows its age in large twisting branches.

Park Drive Ravine is seen from a multi-use trail that was once a road leading into the valley, but it was closed to vehicle traffic in 1973. Unfortunately, on much of the walk, you're relatively far from the ravine slopes and the old oak trees that grow on them, though you can see the characteristic trunk and crown shapes of the oak, which are 150-to-200-years-old. You get closest to the old oak trees as you round the corner to enter the ravine, immediately adjacent to the Don Valley Parkway offramp to Bayview Avenue. The old forest continues on the ravine slope from here to the historic Glen Road bridge. Opposite the start of Milkman's Lane there's a small clearing with some gravel piled up, which happens to be a good lookout to see the twisting, tentacle-like canopy of some very old oak trees in the distance, especially when the leaves are down.

Milkman's Lane leads out of the ravine on the south side. The forest along this old roadway isn't old growth, but at the top, you can stroll through Craigleigh Gardens, a dog park that has scattered old oaks within the park, and some old oak forest on the upper slope adjacent to the park. This is one of few places where you can visit old oaks along the upper slopes, because elsewhere the elaborate Rosedale homes back onto the ravines. Wealthy financier Edmund Osler (who had business ties to Henry Pellatt) lived in a 25-room Victorian home on the site of Craigleigh Gardens until his death in 1924, at which time the property was donated to the city and the home was demolished. Since the home was built in 1876, it's likely that the oaks growing in the park date back at least until then, making them 150-years-old or more.

While you're up there, you may also want to cross the Glen Road bridge for views over the ravine. This bridge was constructed in 1927, replacing the existing bridge at the time (the ornamental iron lattice railing from the old bridge was repurposed as a fence along Avoca Ave). It leads to a swank part of Rosedale beginning with Beaumont Road, an historic street with grand houses that were built in the late 1800s. The ravine side of Beaumont Road offers some views of old-growth oaks when the leaves are off, particularly near several homes that were built into the ravine. Beaumont Road was also the scene of a memorable footnote in rock and roll history.

Number 5 Beaumont Road was owned by Gordon Lightfoot in 1975, when Bob Dylan's "Rolling Thunder Revue" rolled through town. After joining Dylan at the concert at Maple Leaf Gardens, Lightfoot invited the entire cast back to a house party at his Rosedale home. An alcohol- and drug-fuelled party ensued. "I don't remember all that transpired at Gord's, because we drank to excess," recounts Ramblin' Jack Elliott, "but we were told we had quite a lot of fun." Meanwhile, Dylan and Lightfoot, two of the world's great songwriters, played acoustic guitars together in a room upstairs. Nicholas Jennings wrote in his biography of Lightfoot: "After selling out the largest venue in the city, attracting a constellation of music's brightest stars and hosting a fabulously decadent party, all these two artists wanted to do was retreat to a room and trade songs over acoustic guitars. For Lightfoot, as for Dylan, it was always about the song."

Rather than return down Milkman's Lane, you may wish to follow a meandering route through the residential neighbourhoods of Rosedale, via South Drive, Crescent Road, etc., that roughly parallels the ravines. There are charming historic homes along the way, and after many turns you can make your way to the end of Mathersfield Road, where a stairway descends back into the ravine. From here, trails run along the mid-slope of the ravine and take you close to some pockets of old-growth oak forest, including passing right beside some large old oaks. The trails continue all the way to David A. Balfour Park and Avoca Ave (note the historic iron railing while you're there). These trails are best avoided when conditions are icy or muddy, as portions are steep and can be slippery.

The fence at Avoca Ave was moved from the Glen Road bridge in 1927.

Crothers Woods and E.T. Seton Park

✤ What you'll like

These are some of the least disturbed forests on the slopes of the Don River Valley, and they offer a sense of isolation in the heart of Toronto. Here you can retrace the steps of famous naturalists Charles Sauriol and E.T. Seton, among towering 160-year-old oak trees, while catching views of the Toronto skyline through the forest.

✤ How to get there

By car – Thomas Hauser Memorial Trailhead (at the Loblaws, 11 Redway Road, is a good access point. The parking close to the trailhead is for Crothers Woods, further away is for store parking only. There is a dirt parking area near the North Toronto Wastewater Treatment Plant, down a laneway from the Loblaws parking. Another access point is a parking lot in E.T. Seton Park, off Thorncliffe Park Drive (43.703, -79.338), which accesses informal mountain bike trails east of Crothers Woods.

By public transit – It's a short walk to the forest from TTC stops on Millwood Road and Thorncliffe Park Drive. The stairs near Redway and Millwood Roads are near stops for #56 Leaside or #88 South Leaside TTC buses.

By bike – There's good bike access to both E.T. Seton Park and Crothers Woods from the lower Don River Trail, the West Don Trail, or the Lower Don Recreation Trail.

✤ What to do

The hike from Crothers Woods to E.T. Seton Park, or vice versa, makes a nice half-day return trip. The trails are intermediate difficulty with a number of hills and some uneven ground. Bring plenty of water and snacks.

Views of the cityscape through the trees remind us just how urban this old-growth forest really is, as does the distant hum of the Don Valley Parkway.

✤ Learn more

This walk follows the footsteps of Charles Sauriol—a conservationist, beekeeper, and spokesperson for the Don Valley, who left his mark (and books) after having a cabin near this spot for more than four decades. I wondered as I started my hike if I could find the remnants of the cabin. But more on that later; first I had some old forest to see.

Some of the best old-growth forest occurs below the Loblaws and over to the water treatment plant, and there are several trail loops to explore. This forest has old oak trees on the upper slopes that likely reach 150-to-200-years-old. Otherwise, it is dominated by maple and beech, which are mostly under 150-years-old. Many of the beech are infected with beech bark disease (see Bronte Creek page to learn more). Bitternut hickory is also a fairly common tree to watch for, and there's a large, beautiful butternut in the forest to the south-east of the Loblaws. Butternut is an endangered tree in Ontario

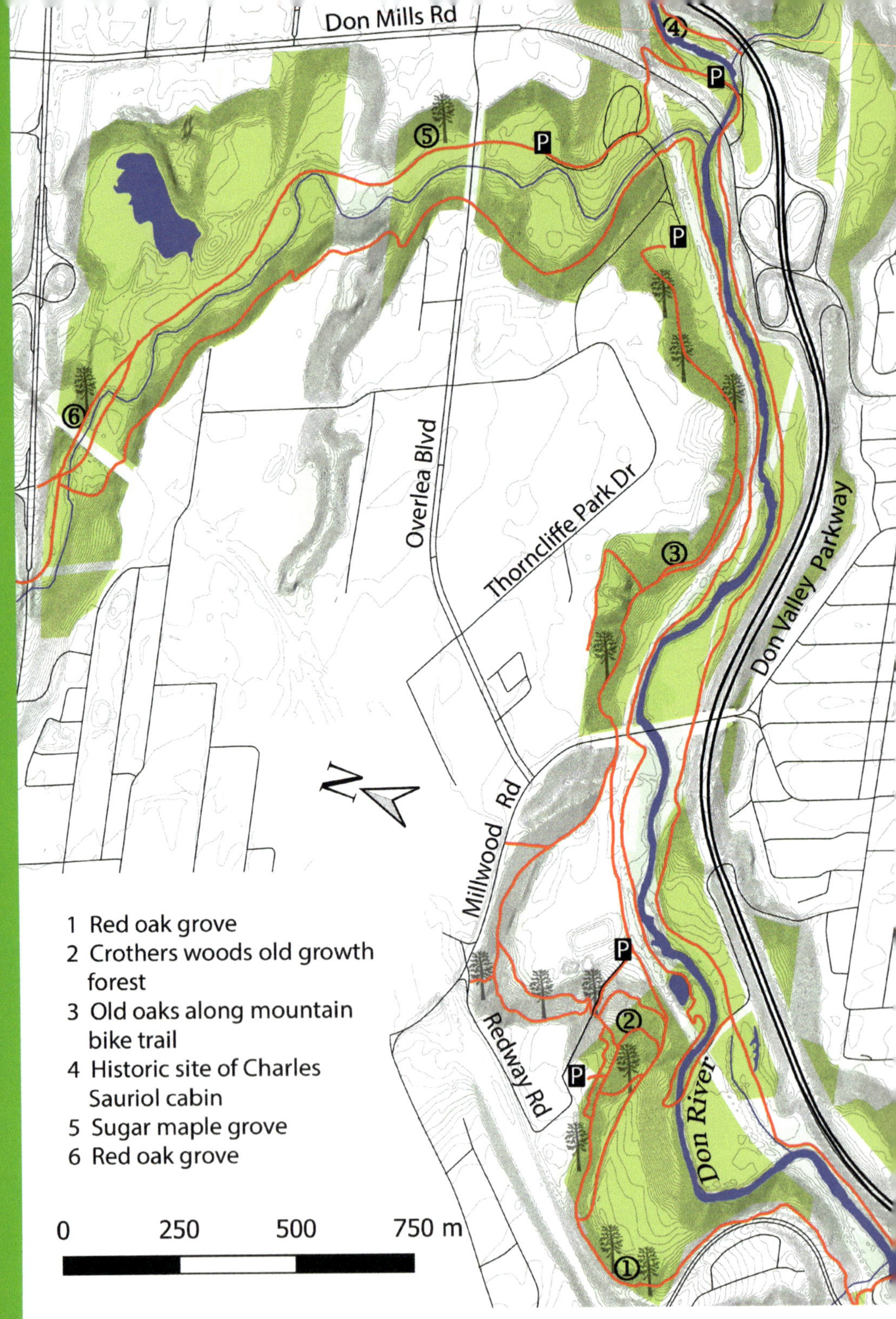
Don Mills Rd
Overlea Blvd
Thorncliffe Park Dr
Don Valley Parkway
Millwood Rd
Redway Rd
Don River
N
1 Red oak grove
2 Crothers woods old growth forest
3 Old oaks along mountain bike trail
4 Historic site of Charles Sauriol cabin
5 Sugar maple grove
6 Red oak grove
0
250
500
750 m

A smurf's eye view of mayapple in Crothers Woods.

because so many have been killed by butternut canker, an introduced fungus that has been killing butternuts in North America since 1967. Seeing an old-growth butternut tree is a rare treat in any forest, particularly in the heart of Canada's largest city. Scattered white pines emerge through the canopy of hardwood trees, and are likely at least as old as the maples.

The old growth at Crothers Woods is well documented, but I was pleasantly surprised by old-growth forest continuing beyond the sewage treatment plant and to the east of Millwood Road. This is essentially a continuation of the Crothers Woods old growth but not advertised as such, and it is mostly known to the local mountain bikers. When I visited, someone had also used the ravine as a dumping ground, with garbage strewn down the slopes near the Thorncliffe Park high-rise apartment buildings. This is a throwback to behaviours of the first half of the 20th century, when the Don Valley was a dumping ground for Toronto's refuse, sewage, and other pollution. The fact that I find this garbage shocking and unusual tells me we've made real progress toward appreciating the natural treasures in our backyards, even if we're not quite there yet.

Of course, this is no longer the valley it once was in the early 1800s. As I make my way past the garbage and toward E.T. Seton Park, there are still many old oaks on the upper ravine slopes, some of which would have started as seedlings roughly between 1820 and 1840. Since that time, countless wildlife species have disappeared from southern Ontario, and E.T. Seton, the naturalist namesake of the park I was walking in, wrote eloquently about many of them. Seton wrote about seeing one of the last great flocks of passenger pigeons, which he witnessed from his home near the Don Valley when he was 15-years-old.

"I shall never forget the last great horde that passed over, it was in 1876 about April 20th. An army of pigeons flew overhead due north. The flocks seemed only about twenty deep but extending east and west as far as could be seen fading into a smoky line on each horizon. There must have been hundreds of thousands in that flock and it was succeeded by others of similar extent every half hour for most of the day. I saw it all from my bedroom window and I must sorrowfully add that it was the last of the great flocks, that according to record, ever came over Toronto."

I find it impossible to reflect on the fate of passenger pigeons without feeling a sense of loss. The last passenger pigeon (Martha) died in the Cincinnati Zoo in 1914, but they had vanished from the wild years before that. Passenger pigeons were once the most abundant bird in North America, numbering in the billions. It is estimated that before European colonization, one out of every four birds on the continent was a passenger pigeon. Their diet was mostly the nuts of beech, oak, hickory, and chestnut, and they moved in massive flocks to get to nesting grounds. Many trees have "mast years" when huge crops of nuts are produced across large forest areas. This is what the pigeons were seeking out by the millions.

A rare old-growth butternut. The flattened ridges on the bark often criss-cross, resulting in characteristic canoe shapes that can help identify the tree.

Near where I live, their imprint on the land is memorialized in the town name Omemee (their name in Ojibwe) and Pigeon Lake. What happened to them? It was a combination of habitat loss and overhunting on a massive scale that drove them to extinction. The former concentrated the birds into ever smaller areas where hunting was easy, where every last bird that was found was netted, clubbed, or shot, to be sold in the growing cities of the 19th century. The old oaks at Crothers Woods were already moderate-sized trees when that last flock passed over in 1876; you may want to take a few minutes to imagine what it would have been like to experience a flock flying overhead, one of the great natural wonders of the world.

As you approach E.T. Seton Park, you'll pass some dead trees near the trail, which are valuable habitat for some of the modern wildlife species of the Don Valley, especially the pileated woodpecker. There are large oblong feeding cavities on some of the trees where the woodpeckers have gone after carpenter ants, their favourite food. Curious to think that pileated woodpeckers are really just flying anteaters, but there it is. They play an important role in creating nest cavities for themselves that are often reused by others. They are one of nature's great home builders, though rarely credited for it.

While many of the animals Seton wrote about have declined or vanished, there is one he worried about needlessly: raccoons. These curious masked creatures naturally den in hollow trees, and by the late 1800s these were very rare in the Don Valley. This combined with hunting nearly extirpated the clever omnivorous animals from the Valley, and Seton expressed concern for their future. As we now know, raccoons are highly intelligent and adaptable creatures who can look out for themselves. Charles Sauriol, an admirer of Seton, wrote in 1984 that "Up until the 1960's raccoons were respectable, law-abiding types with a folksy, country manner. They roamed the valley at night looking for tidbits such as crayfish, minnows,

Occasionally there are reminders that, yes, you are still in the city.

frogs, toads, insects and whatever else raccoons fancy." By 1984, however, Sauriol describes them stealing a hamburger out of a neighbour's hand, spreading garbage across lawns, and generally treating humans with disdain should they acknowledge them at all. And denning in hollow trees is great, but in the city why not try a chimney? Or attic, storm sewer, crawl space, etc. Yes, raccoons are doing just fine.

The trail comes out on a road and parking lot. This is a good spot to turn around. On my visit, I had one more objective, though: to look for the remains of Sauriol's cabin, and the grove of trees that he planted. Sauriol himself was an important figure for conservation in Toronto, and the first director of the Nature Conservancy of Canada, but most people today know little about him. He became intimately connected with the Don Valley, first as a boy scout, then by renting a cottage that he later bought, and finally by fighting and working to protect at least some of the nature that he had come to know and love. The changes he witnessed in the valley, and how

These sections of railway track once supported a suspension bridge built by Charles Sauriol.

it shaped his ideas on conservation are recorded in his books. He wrote in 1984 that "the feeling the valley once had, of being a wild, isolated place, is gone. But," he went on, "who knows? Without the efforts of the D.V.C.A. [Don Valley Conservation Association] the greenbelt may have never matured to what we know today." And indeed, without Sauriol and many, many others like him, we wouldn't have the modern vision of the Greenbelt, which goes beyond even what Sauriol imagined. Sauriol could be proud, as can the many who came both before and after him, and those yet to come. The Greenbelt will always need its defenders.

I never did find the cabin, and the grove of trees he planted is gone, perhaps a victim of the construction of the parkway. But I did find one clue that he was once there. If you wander along the east bank of the Don River, upstream from Taylor Massey Creek, through dense thickets of vegetation and a fog of mosquitoes, eventually you may stumble on two parallel sections of rusted railway track sticking vertically out of the ground. Some cables hanging from them hint at their one-time function: they were the anchors to support a suspension foot bridge that Sauriol used to cross the Don River. Maybe one day there will be a trail to the spot and a plaque honouring Sauriol's cabin. For me, nothing could beat the thrill of stumbling through the brush, pursued by hundreds of mosquitoes, and suddenly finding them, monuments to an icon of conservation.

West Don Valley (Sunnybrook Park and Wilket Creek)

✤ What you'll like

Sunnybrook and the surrounding parks cover several hundred hectares of greenspace in the heart of Toronto, with old-growth forest scattered throughout. The Thomas H. Thomson Nature Trails, straddling Sunnybrook and Wilket Creek Parks, meander through impressive old white, red, and bur oak trees. This is one of the few places in Toronto where old forest grows on a plateau instead of a ravine slope, which makes for larger trees. Nearby Glendon Forest is crisscrossed by mountain-bike trails that allow an intimate visit with the forest for those of us on foot. Altogether this huge urban greenspace is an island of cool shade on a hot summer day.

✤ How to get there

By car – There are many parking lots in Sunnybrook Park, any one of which could be used to explore old-growth forest. The main entrance is at 1132 Leslie Street (just north of Eglinton), which accesses most of the parking lots. It is also possible to reach the westernmost parking via the Sunnybrook Health Sciences Centre, but it is taking a chance, since this small parking lot may be full. There is also parking at Toronto Botanical Gardens, Glendon College, and some street parking near Serena Gundy Park.

By public transit – There are many ways to reach the parks by TTC. Buses #51 and #54 follow Leslie Street along the edge of Wilket Creek and Sunnybrook Parks, with several possible stops (e.g., Stop ID: 5440, 14957, or 14965). Bus #11 on Bayview will bring you near the west side of the park (e.g., stops 1713, 1717), which is also near the old-growth forest at Sherwood Park. You could also walk to some of the old growth in under an hour from Eglinton or Lawrence subway stations.

A bridge over the West Don River will take you from the parking lot to a small pocket of old growth in Serena Gundy Park.

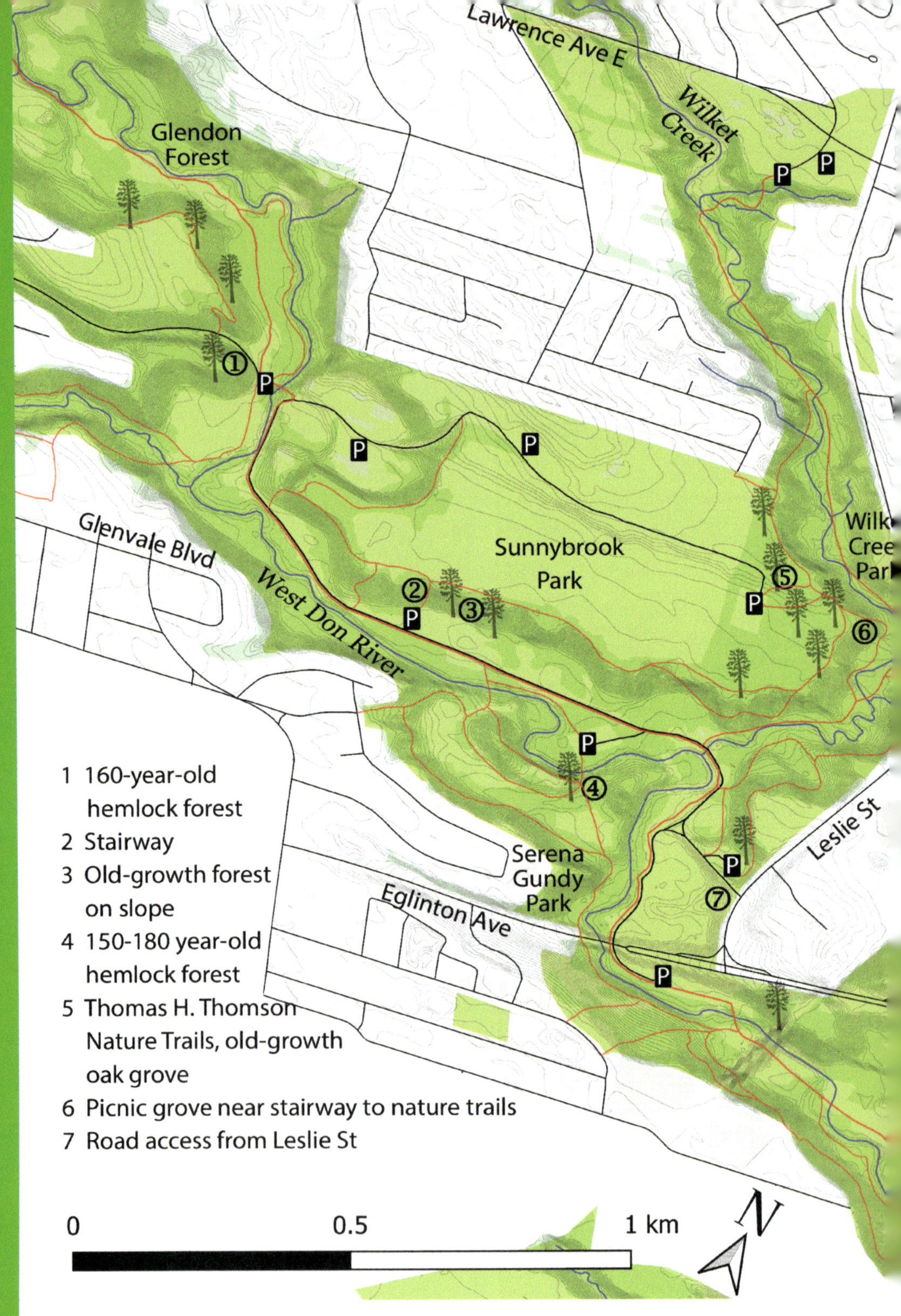
Lawrence Ave E
Wilket Creek
Glendon Forest
P
Sunnybrook Park
Wilket Creek Park
Glenvale Blvd
West Don River
Serena Gundy Park
Eglinton Ave
Leslie St
1 160-year-old hemlock forest
2 Stairway
3 Old-growth forest on slope
4 150-180 year-old hemlock forest
5 Thomas H. Thomson Nature Trails, old-growth oak grove
6 Picnic grove near stairway to nature trails
7 Road access from Leslie St
0
0.5
1 km
N

By bike – Bicycle is a natural way to get there, depending on where you're coming from. For example, from Union Station you could reach Sunnybrook by bike in under an hour, with most of your trip being along bike trails in the Don Valley. Having a bike with you could also allow you to explore more of the park. There are several Bike Share locations within Sunnybrook and adjacent parks, as well as at E.T. Seton and Evergreen Brick Works.

✤ What to do

You can make a very nice loop along the ridge top from the nature trails at Wilket Creek to the long stairway at Sunnybrook Park. Descend the stairs and cross the first bridge over the West Don River, walk through some old forest in Serena Gundy, before crossing back over the West Don. Then return via roads and multi-use trail, or back along the ridge. There are several parking lots or access points that would make good starting points along this loop. There are also forests to explore near Sunnybrook Health Sciences Centre and Glendon Forest. Bring food and water and remember to stop and enjoy benches along the way.

While you're in the area, you may want to visit Sherwood Park's old-growth forest, which is one of Toronto's most impressive (be aware it is a dog off-leash area). If you're on bike, you can also include either Crothers Woods or Rosedale Ravines into your day. At the latter, you could stop for a bite at Evergreen Brick Works.

✤ Learn more

I arrived at Wilket Creek by bike, using Toronto's fantastic system of bike paths, and left with tired feet after hours of hiking. On my return trip, the low sun cast long shadows on the grass, and groups of families and friends had gathered around barbecues in E.T. Seton Park. Parks like this really are community gathering spaces, making the many surrounding apartment buildings seem far more enviable. In fact, during summer heatwaves, Toronto's ravines can literally be life savers, islands of cool in a city so hot that the number of deaths increases. Other parts of the city, where there are few trees and a lot of asphalt and concrete, are heat islands where air temperatures can be as much as 8 to 12 degrees Celsius hotter than in greenspaces.

On urbanheatislands.com there's a map of heat distribution in Toronto, showing the coolest parts of the city as a light green, while the hottest are red to purple. Here the network of parks shows as rivers and oases of green dissecting the city. A study of Canada's cities found that recently Toronto averaged about 12 very hot days a year (temperature over 30 degrees C) but that is predicted to rise to 30 days a year as early as 2040, and could reach 60 days a year by the end of the century, if we keep emitting large amounts of greenhouse gases. I hope we'll get our act together before that happens because it sounds like Hell, literally.

But whatever our future, we need to be mindful of how we design our cities. Toronto heat islands are still growing at an estimated 3% a year. Green roofs and street trees can make a big difference, by increasing shade while storing moisture and releasing it from plant leaves on hot days, causing evaporative cooling (similar to how sweat cools our bodies). Adding or retaining greenspace also has a huge impact, creating sanctuaries for people and animals to go to, while also cooling the surrounding neighbourhoods.

Greenspaces in cities are not a new idea. They have existed since the first cities were formed but have always been monopolized to some extent by the wealthy and the powerful. Many parks that exist today were once the exclusive private gardens of royalty and aristocracy. For example, the Royal Parks in London (including Hyde Park and Kensington Gardens) add hundreds of hectares of greenspace that were once the exclusive preserve of The Royal Family.

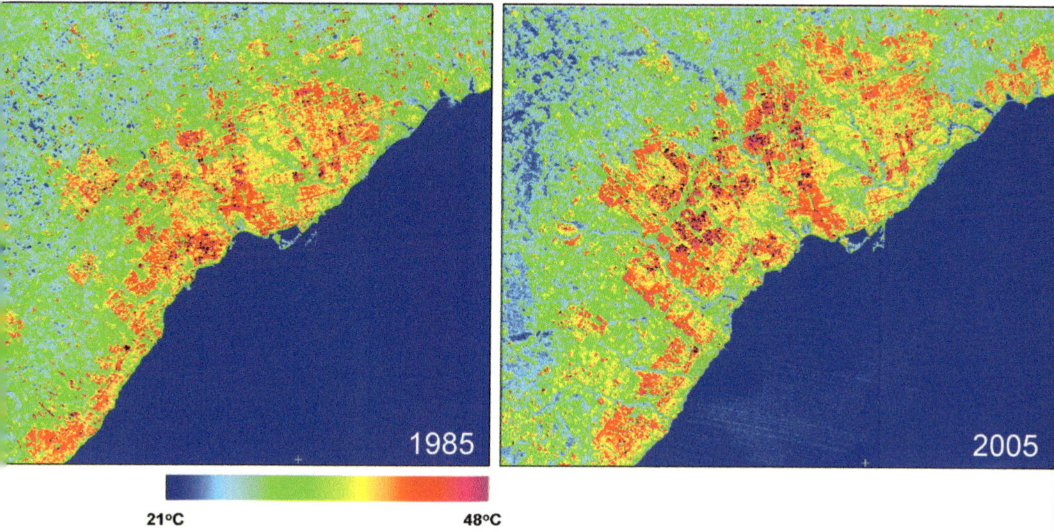

Surface temperatures of the Greater Toronto Area in 1985 (left) and 2005 (right) show how heat islands have grown along with the city. A pleasant mid-20s day under forest cover can translate to an unbearable 48 degrees Celsius in some dense urban areas. Reprinted with permission from Zhang, Y. and Sun, L. 2019.

The same is true to a lesser extent in Toronto. We didn't have a royal family, but we did have a wealthy elite who owned country estates on the edge of, and soon contained within, a rapidly growing city. One of the largest was the Kilgour estate. Joseph Kilgour was known for his love of horseback riding but had made his money by co-founding the Canada Paper Company. Alice Kilgour donated the property to the city in 1928, and it became Sunnybrook Park. The adjacent Gundy estate was donated in 1960 to form Serena Gundy Park. Toronto Botanical Gardens is on the former estate of Rupert Edwards, who sold it to the city in 1954. The Wood estate became Glendon Forest and the Glendon campus of York University. These former estates and Wilket Creek Park add around 285 hectares of public greenspace near the heart of Toronto, with additional parks in the connected ravines.

It still helps to have money if you want to live around here. I remember the first time I accidentally drove into the Bridle Path neighbourhood just north of Sunnybrook, not realizing that Lawrence Avenue East is interrupted at Bayview (before the days of universal GPS navigation). I couldn't believe the mansions and estates that surrounded me. The Bridle Path earned its name by being part of the riding grounds of the adjacent estates, and today it includes the home of Drake. Gordon Lightfoot and Prince once lived there, as did Conrad Black. Lightfoot, apart from being Canada's musical storyteller through the 60s and 70s, and a bona fide rock star (the documentary about his life is worth watching), loved Canada's landscape and performed at a benefit concert to save Temagami old-growth forest in 1989. I wonder if he knew about the old-growth forest at the end of the street where he lived until his death in 2023.

I locked my bike and started my walk from the trail to the Botanical Gardens. Just before the multi-use trail crosses the first bridge over Wilket Creek (43.7239, -79.3503) there are some dirt walking trails that cut off to the west, toward Sunnybrook Park. From there the trail climbs through some middle-aged hemlock forest and tall white pines, on stairs made from dug-in cedar logs. The stairs are still in reasonable condition despite probably irregular maintenance, a testament to traditional backcountry trail building techniques. At the top of the hill there's a four-way junction with a sign for the Thomas H. Thomson Nature Trails. Not to be confused with Tom Thomson the painter (as I initially thought), though that Tom Thomson also might have rambled through this forest when he lived in Toronto in the early 20th century.

From this junction, pretty much all trails lead through forest that reaches about 150-years-old, and scattered through it are large red, white, and occasional bur oaks that may reach 180-years-old or more. At the north end (where the trail runs into the posh neighbourhoods adjacent to the Bridle Path) there are some old bleached white pine snags. Walking the other way along the ravine rim, there is old forest alternating with younger forest all

A large red oak in Sunnybrook Park, a short walk from Drake's mansion and, until recently, Gordon Lightfoot's home

These delightful signs along the Thomas H. Thomson trails suggest nature-based exercises from another era.

the way to the stairs in Sunnybrook Park (where there is also hardwood forest that's at least 130-years-old). A dirt trail runs just inside the forest edge, parallel to a horse trail in the field. Although these aren't necessarily the oldest trees, the forest walk along the ridge is one of my favourite walks in the area.

From the stairs, it would be possible to walk the road back for a loop; you could cross the bridge to Serena Gundy, where a tiny pocket of hemlock forest reaches over 150-years-old (43.7191, -79.3549), or head toward Glendon Forest where old-growth forest curves around the ridge below Sunnybrook Health Sciences Centre. The latter is mostly accessed by informal mountain bike trails. The trails are a little rough, and have impacts, but offer an intimate walk through the forest.

Rouge National Urban Park

✤ What you'll like

This is a huge natural park near the heart of the GTA. Highlights include mature maple and hemlock forest, remnant oaks from old savannah forest, and a dramatic walk along a narrow "hog's back" ridge between two rivers.

✤ How to get there

By car – The Mast Trail can be reached by exiting from Kingston Road at Glen Rouge campground. Parking for the trailhead is just before the entrance to the campground. From there, cross a foot bridge to the east side of the Rouge and hike upstream along the Mast Trail.

The Woodlands Trail is off Reesor Road just south of Steeles Avenue East.

By public transit – From Rouge Hill GO station, you can get to Rouge Park on TTC by taking bus #85A; exit at Shephard Avenue and Kingston Road, and walk 1.2 km. Or take Durham Transit 900 Kingston Road/Hwy 2, exit at Altona, and walk 750m to Glen Rouge (roughly an hour and a quarter in total from Union Station).

By bike – Glen Rouge is only a short bike ride from the Waterfront Trail, via Dyson Road and Rougemount Drive.

✤ What to do

You could spend a few hours wandering on the Mast Trail, including some side trails and digressions. There is ample opportunity to continue exploring on the extensive trail system. A pleasant day could include a bike ride on the waterfront trail and a few hours of hiking on Rouge Park Trails. You could also make a reservation to camp at the Glen Rouge Campground.

The beginning of the Mast Trail is a steep climb through shady hemlock forest.

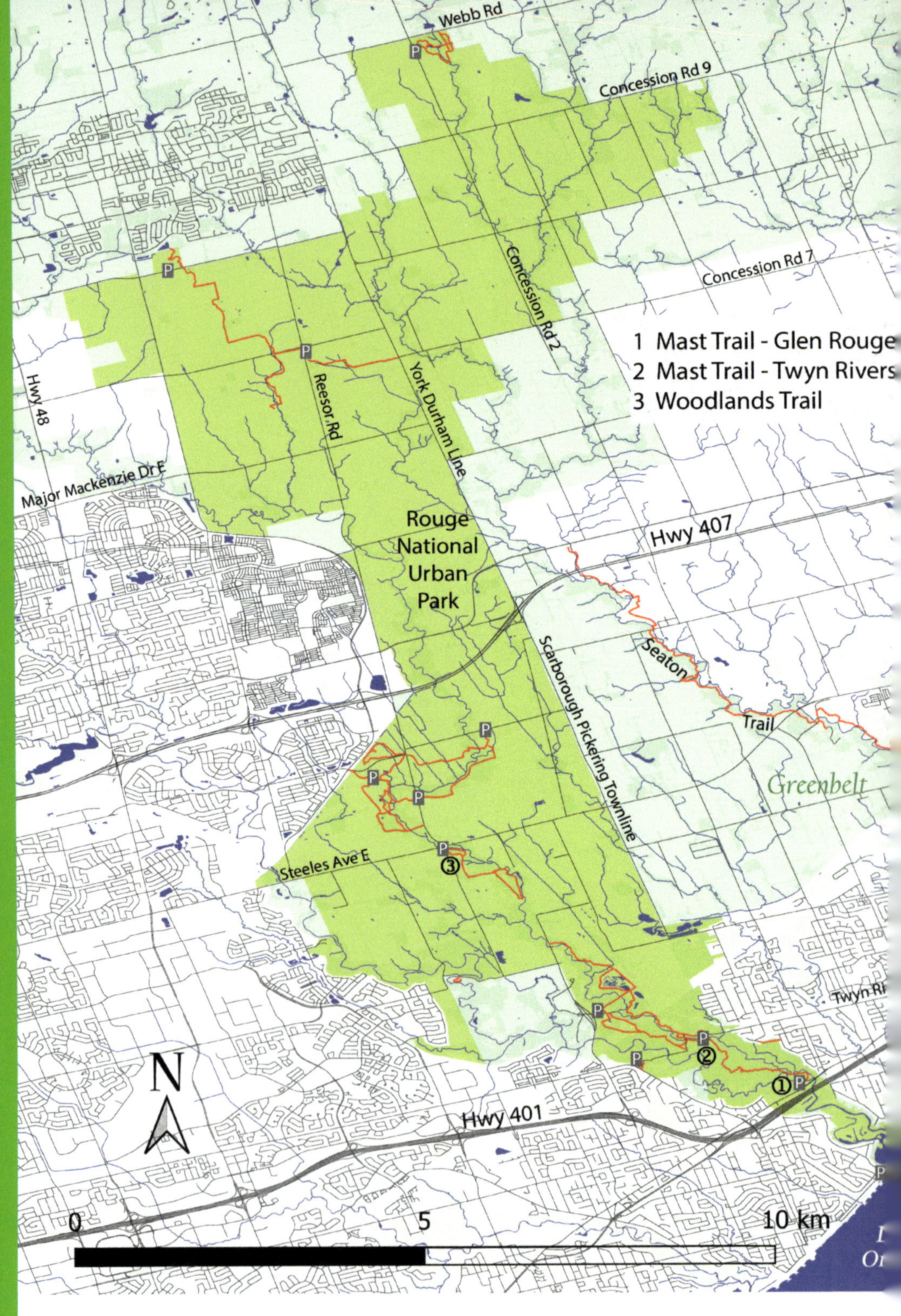

Webb Rd
Concession Rd 9
Concession Rd 7
Concession Rd 2
1 Mast Trail - Glen Rouge
2 Mast Trail - Twyn Rivers
3 Woodlands Trail
Hwy 48
Reesor Rd
York Durham Line
Major Mackenzie Dr E
Rouge
National
Urban
Park
Hwy 407
Seaton
Trail
Scarborough Pickering Townline
Greenbelt
Steeles Ave E
N
Hwy 401
0
5
10 km

✤ Learn more

The Rouge Valley sneaks up on you unexpectedly. If you drive into Toronto from the east on highway 401, you pass seemingly endless suburbs, but just as you're entering the urban heart of Canada (also the fourth largest city in North America), BAM! There's a beautiful, forested valley. Thirty seconds later (or thirty minutes depending on traffic), you're wondering if it were really there, or some kind of psychosis that makes us see what we most need: sweet, blessed nature! It's even more fun on the GO train. The change isn't quite as stark (the lakeshore is a curious mix of greenspace and neighbourhoods that time forgot), but the wetlands at the mouth of the Rouge, broad marshes waving in the wind with tall pines on the slopes behind, are something else!

Rouge National Urban Park was created by a series of unfortunate and fortunate events. Three stand out: the devastation of Hurricane Hazel, the boondoggle of the Pickering airport lands, and, finally, the Save the Rouge campaign.

Hurricane Hazel was the deadliest hurricane of the 1954 season. After killing 469 people in Haiti and 95 people in the USA, it hit Canada, and 81 people were killed in flooding when 28cm of rain fell in less than two days. Three thousand people were left homeless, and the course of Toronto's development was changed forever as Toronto expropriated river valleys (including the Rouge) for floodplain protection. The worst of the destruction was along the Humber, but urban development changed for all of Toronto, and to some extent Ontario.

Another big year was 1972, when the Government of Canada expropriated 75 sq km of land on the boundary of Pickering and Scarborough (known as the Pickering Lands) to develop a new airport. By 1975 the airport was put on hold indefinitely (more about this in the Seaton Trail section of this book), and since then the federal government has been

Rouge Park preserves tracts of natural forest on the edge of dense urbanization. Here some white pines grow in the valley with ostrich fern.

leasing properties on the Pickering Lands back to residential, farm, and commercial tenants. Rouge National Urban Park owes 4000 hectares (almost 2/3 of the park) to the airport lands.

Meanwhile, the river valleys and floodplains that had been bought by the city after Hurricane Hazel had grown tremendously in value. Developers had their eye on them, and in the late 1980s, under pressure from the Ontario Realty Corporation, Scarborough city councillors started talking about rezoning 5000 acres of Rouge land for subdivisions. The Metropolitan Toronto and Region Conservation Authority weighed in, saying that the table land was above the flood plain and didn't need to be conserved. But the fight was on, as members of Save the Rouge Valley System (SRVS), including Glenn de Baeremaeker (a future city councillor) and Lois James, stepped in to harness public opinion against the proposal. "It will be up to us to make the politicians and government agencies change their vision and widen the greenbelt corridor beyond the flood area," James told a *Toronto Star* reporter at the time. By the time a vote was held on the measure, it was defeated 14 to 1.

Years of effort ensued, culminating in 2015 when the Rouge National Urban Park was created by the federal Conservative government, then strengthened by the incoming Liberals. Ecological integrity is now the primary guiding principle in this massive urban park. There will still be a lot of work to protect it from invasive species, trampling, and other threats unique to urban parks, but the Rouge has proven to be resilient in the past.

The Mast Trail is one of the best places to see old-growth forest in the Park, and it is said to be the remnants of an historic logging route. Centuries ago, large pine trees were dragged out by oxen to be used as masts for the British Navy. Today the forest is second growth; you are seeing trees that mostly regrew after logging. Few, if any, of the trees are likely to be over 200-years-old, but the forest is once again entering the old-growth stage, with many trees reaching 120-to 180-years-old. It will be centuries yet before it attains its former grandeur, with trees as large as the ones used as masts for the royal navy, but as an urban natural area, Rouge Park is already exceptional, with its large tracts of forest and patches of old growth.

After a short trek from the parking lot, you'll find yourself in a shady oasis, climbing stairs through 120- to 130-year-old hemlock and sugar maple forest with occasional large white and red oak trees. The older oak trees reach 150-to 180-years-old, but most of the forest around them is relatively young. In places, there are occasional white pines growing singly or in groves. White pines tend to be taller than the hardwoods commonly found here, and tower above them as "supercanopy" trees. They have special importance to wildlife, including some species of bats that hunt for insects that congregate around the emergent pine trees.

On its northern half, the Mast Trail follows a narrow hog's back ridge, cut between the Rouge and Little Rouge rivers. The occasional large white and red oaks suggest that the ridge may have formerly been dominated by oak savannah. If you keep your eyes open, you may also spot wild rye, a savannah grass, growing on the ridge. Invasive dog-strangling vine is a problem here and is likely getting worse.

One of the most charming and oldest forest groves on the Mast Trail is at the Twyn Rivers trailhead. The forest has a diverse overstory of hemlock, white pine, sugar maple, and red oak. The average age of the trees is probably around 140 years, but some trees, especially the sugar maples, may approach 200-years-old. The understory is a delightful, diverse fern garden. Look for bulblet fern, ostrich fern, marginal wood fern, intermediate wood fern, and sensitive fern. Some dog-strangling vine is moving in at the edges. Soil disturbance and increased light tend to make this worse, which is why it's especially common along the trails.

A dead tree near the Twyn Rivers trailhead provides food and habitat for many species, including pileated woodpeckers that made the large cavities near its top.

The Seaton Trail

✤ What you'll like

The Seaton Trail is one of southern Ontario's hidden gems. A sometimes strenuous hike in and out of the valley offers spectacular views alternating with quiet oases of nature. West Duffins Creek is remarkably undeveloped, offering a glimpse into what rural Pickering looked like 50 years ago. A few old-growth forests are found along the trail, with trees at least 200-years-old—and scattered old trees mingle with a wide variety of fields and forests along the route. You'll break a sweat to see it; parts of the trail are challenging.

✤ How to get there

By car – There are several trailheads with good parking; from north to south these are: Highway 7 (43.9019, -79.177), Whitevale Road at Mutual Street (43.886, -79.163); Forestream Trail, off Whites Road North (43.869, -79.132); Concession 3, at the Pickering Dog Park (43.864, -79.098). The trail can also be accessed via Valley Farm Road/Old Wildwood Trail.

By public transit – You can reach the southernmost access to the Seaton Trail by bus, exiting at Finch and Valley Farm Road. Walk about 500m up Valley Farm Road to the trailhead at 43.852, -79.087, the junction of Valley Farm Road and "old wildwood trail" on Google Maps. From Union Station, a mix of train and bus will get you to this trailhead in just over an hour.

By bike – The southern trailhead at Valley Farm Road is only about 4 km from the Waterfront Trail. The Greenbelt Cycle Route runs within about 10 km of the northern access points.

✤ What to do

The most spectacular stretch of the Seaton Trail is between Forestream Trail and Whitevale. However you may also want to climb the impressive

The view from the lookout north of Taunton Road is one of the Seaton Trail's many delights.

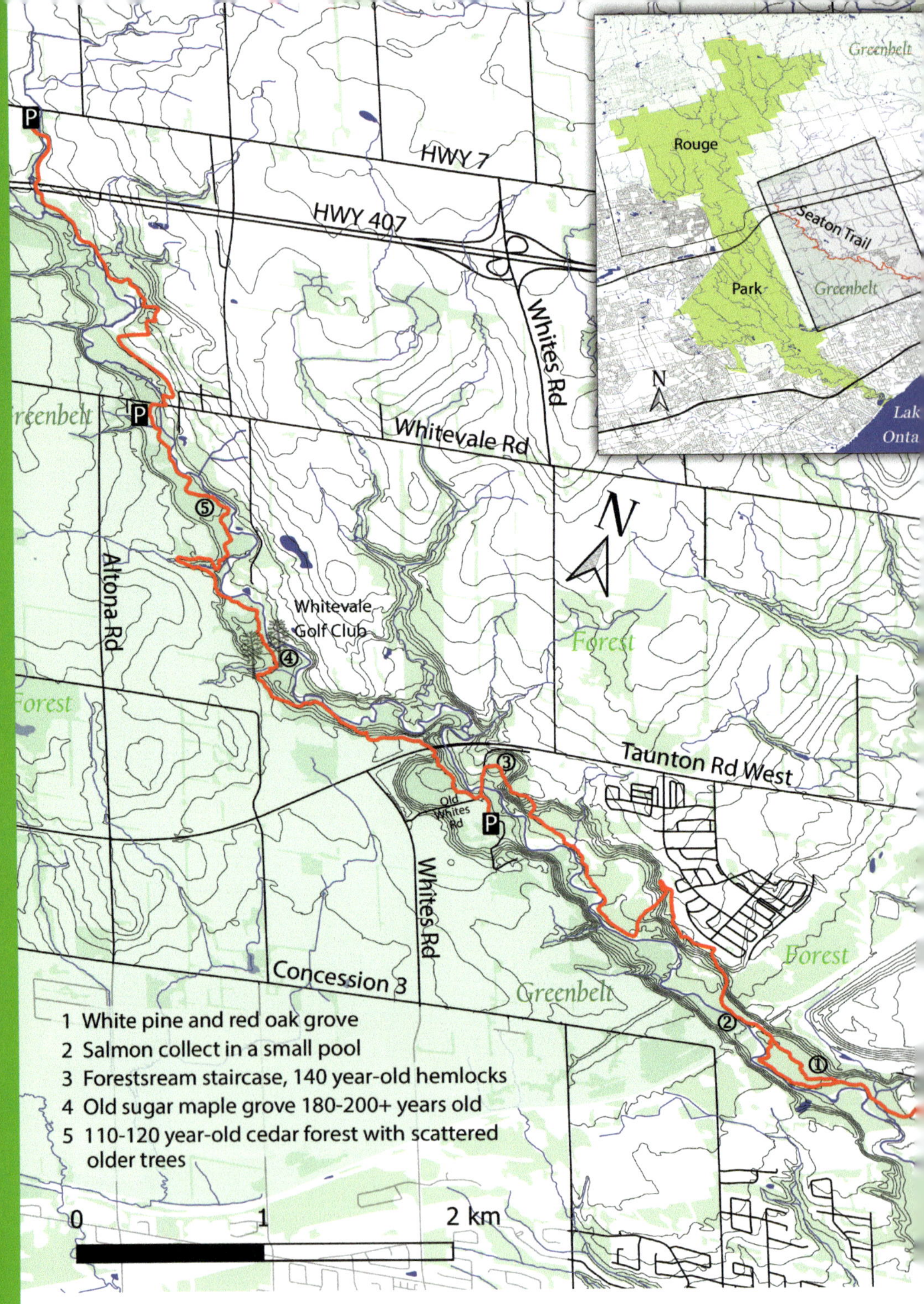
HWY 7
HWY 407
Whites Rd
Whitevale Rd
Greenbelt
Altona Rd
Whitevale Golf Club
Forest
Taunton Rd West
Old Whites Rd
Whites Rd
Concession 3
Greenbelt
Forest
N
Rouge
Park
Seaton Trail
Greenbelt
Lak
Onta
1 White pine and red oak grove
2 Salmon collect in a small pool
3 Forestsream staircase, 140 year-old hemlocks
4 Old sugar maple grove 180-200+ years old
5 110-120 year-old cedar forest with scattered older trees
0
1
2 km

staircase heading downstream (off the closed section of Whites Road North). Whether you start at the north or the south end of this section, it will require backtracking, unless you can set up a shuttle (in which case, if you have the time and energy, try for the whole trail!).

✤ Learn more

The Mississauga (Michi Saagig) people are known as the people of the river mouths. For thousands of years, families congregated at the outlets of the creeks along Lake Ontario in the spring and fall to fish. This was also an important social gathering time for Indigenous families who were more dispersed on the landscape the rest of the year. The most abundant food source in early autumn was Atlantic salmon returning to the creeks to spawn. They were hunted with spears, sometimes at night, using torches made by wedging birch bark into a forked stick.

In 1777 an Irish immigrant by the name of Duffin built a cabin at a creek mouth on the shore of Lake Ontario, in what is now Pickering, to trade for furs with the Mississauga. Though he was a tiny part of the history of this place, and otherwise largely forgotten, he is immortalized in the name of the creek. Running along the west branch of Duffins Creek is the beautiful Seaton Trail.

Traditional trails led inland from the mouths of the rivers of Lake Ontario, and it's likely that some parts of the Seaton Trail follow an ancient route up West Duffins Creek, but how much or which parts I'll leave to your imagination. And it's certainly a trail that inspires the imagination, climbing in and out of the valley at many points, with spectacular views from the tops of steep landslides (please stay behind the barriers). The trail was envisioned and built in the 1970s, around the same time that thousands of hectares of land were expropriated for an airport that would never be built. It was part of the same vision as Mirabel airport north of Montreal, which opened in 1975.

Mirabel was an airport of superlatives, though not necessarily good ones: largest airport in the world in surface size; the most expensive in Canadian history; and very far from the city. Too far, in fact. The last passenger flight left Mirabel in 2004, less than 30 years after it was built. The passenger terminal was demolished between 2014 and 2016, but not before it was the set for a number of movies and commercials. The abandoned airport must have felt a bit haunting to work in, frequented by the ghosts of millions of travellers.

In light of the Mirabel fiasco, it may be just as well that the Pickering airport idea was put on indefinite hold. But the legacy of the Pickering airport lives on in vast tracts of greenspace. Rouge National Urban Park owes 4000 hectares (almost 2/3 of the park!) to the federal airport lands.

At the same time, the provincial government (apparently not wanting to miss out on angering a large group of farmers) expropriated land south of the federal airport lands to create a planned community of Seaton, to "service" the airport, whatever that means. When the airport was put on hold, it had the effect of locking the land away so that it couldn't be developed. Because it's surrounded primarily by forests and fields, not asphalt roads and asphalt roofs, Duffins Creek today has some of the best water quality of any of the GTA rivers, and has populations of rare and endangered fish.

On the east side of the Seaton Trail, about half of the so-called Seaton Lands were recently slated for development, now underway, while the other half is to remain greenspace. Most likely, water quality in West Duffins Creek will decline as housing is built along its east side. The west of the creek was slated for permanent protection as the Duffins–Rouge Agricultural Preserve, an important part of the Greenbelt.

In late December 2022, Doug Ford's Conservative government decided to open up the Duffins Rouge Agricultural Preserve to housing, which would have threatened the high water quality of the creek and meant houses could be built up to the edge of the Seaton Trail. Thankfully, after more than half a year of criticism and scandal, the government reversed this very unpopular decision.

Concession 3 to Forestream Trail

The forest on this section of the trail is not as old as the section to the north, but there are a few highlights. Along the Woods Side Trail there are some white pine, red oak, and hemlock that are not quite old growth, but will be if we wait a couple of decades. Further up, after crossing under a large railway trestle and some new culvert work, there are the foundations of an old railway trestle, part of the Canadian Northern Railway. In September and October salmon collect in the pool beside the old concrete pier; it's impressive to see dozens of the very large fish, and you can appreciate the food resource salmon would have been for countless generations of Indigenous people.

The trail continues past the development of New Seaton. With storm water management techniques, including collection ponds, this and future developments will test the sustainability of urban development, and whether it's compatible with fish like brook trout, red-sided dace, and Atlantic salmon.

My favourite feature on this stretch of trail is the large metal staircase winding down the hill to the closed portion of Whites Road North. The hemlock forest through which it descends is around 140-years-old; it's just becoming an old-growth forest. Descending the stairs almost feels like walking through the forest canopy. To reach the northbound trail, cross Duffins Creek on Whites Road North and watch for the trail on the far side.

Forestream Trail to Whitevale

The trail heading north climbs again, then crosses under Taunton Road and soon reaches a spectacular viewpoint over the valley that is one of the

The staircase descending to Old Whites Trail

highlights of the trail. When the trail descends back into the valley, there is once again some old-ish forest on the slope, with maples probably reaching 140-years-old or so, then back into a typical young floodplain forest, mostly white cedar. After a few more ups and downs, you'll arrive at a true pocket of old-growth forest.

The trail descends parallel to a pretty tributary valley overhung by mature hemlocks, and then a bridge crosses the small tributary stream. After crossing the bridge, watch for a charismatic sugar maple across the stream on the right. Winnifred Wake, in her book *A Nature Guide to Ontario,* describes the Seaton Trail as having 300- to 400-year-old sugar maples, but gives no more information. After contacting Wake for more details, I eventually came to the realization that no one, including Wake herself,

This old sugar maple near the Seaton Trail has a growth form that's often compared to a celery stalk.

Bark balding at the base of an old sugar maple

knows exactly which trees this refers to. It is third-hand information, but that doesn't mean it's untrue. And I could believe this maple tree is 300-years-old, with its tall ropey trunk and massive upper limbs. This growth form with the big limbs clustered at the top, is sometimes compared to a celery stalk. Along with the corded trunk, it's a good indicator of old age.

The trail runs through a significant grove of old-growth forest just after this. Keep an eye out for balding bark on sugar maples, and large branches high on the trees, both signs of old age. The old trees here are not quite as obvious as that first tree, but are still impressive. Mixed in are a few old hemlocks. There were once beech trees, but they've all been killed by beech bark disease. It's a small forest patch but quite beautiful, with a lot of 150- to 200-year-old trees. This is the only place the Whitevale Golf Course crosses Duffins Creek (it can be seen from the trail when leaves are down), and they actually cut some of the old-growth trees to make the hole. Some logs are piled near the edge, also some "slab" offcuts left over from milling trees with a portable sawmill. I think the cutting of the old growth happened during a golf course renovation from 2004–2006, and it emphasizes the need to identify and conserve our old-growth forests, much like we do our heritage buildings.

As the trail leaves the grove, it drops onto the floodplain. A few more very old cedars give way to extensive middle-aged (100- to 120-year-old) cedar forest, mixed with hemlock. There's not much to mention about it except the profusion of ferns, the mossy understory, and vibrant green that seems to glow at certain times of day. On the planning maps, the Whitevale Bypass is scheduled to cross this section of the valley. I can only hope it is never built.

Oak Ridges Moraine

Humber Valley Heritage Trail, Bolton tract

⁜ What you'll like

A picturesque mix of farm fields and forest borders, the Humber Valley Heritage Trail reminds us that protection of farmland is an important function of Ontario's Greenbelt. Pockets of old-growth forest are interspersed with fields and abandoned orchards, beautiful vistas, and fantastical old open-grown "wolf" trees. This Trail is one of Ontario's little known gems, but it can be physically demanding, with the trail often climbing in and out of the valley.

⁜ How to get there

By car – Parking is available at Dicks Dam and Edelweiss parks on Glasgow Road in Bolton, at Emil Kolb Pkwy, or off Castlederg Side Road.

By public transit – From downtown Bolton, it is less than a 15-minute walk to the trailhead on Glasgow Road (across from Deer Valley Drive 43.8797, -79.7500). From Toronto, it's little more than an hour on the GO bus (or combination of train and bus) to Bolton.

View across the Humber Valley

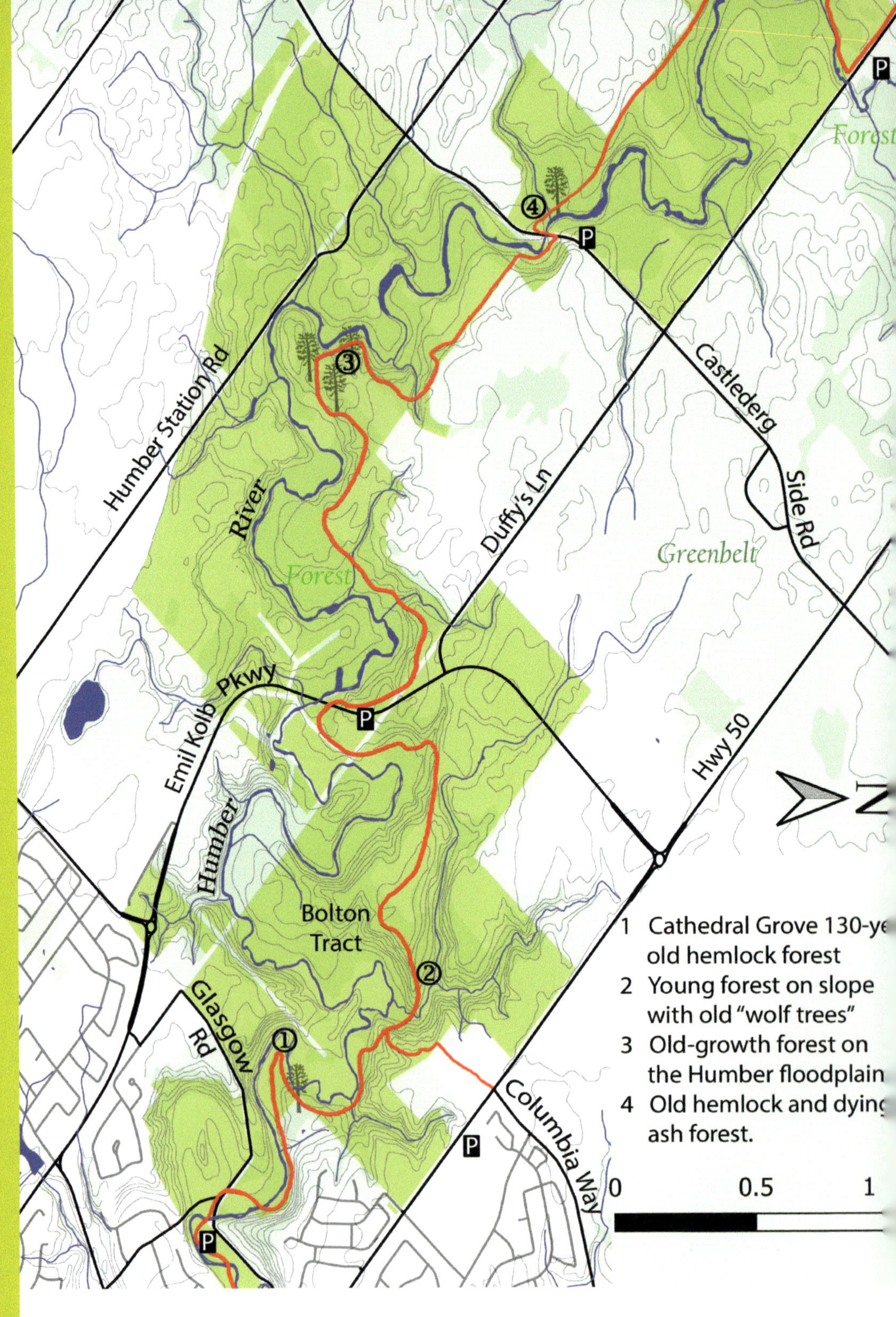

Forest
Castlederg
Side Rd
Humber Station Rd
River
Duffy's Ln
Greenbelt
Forest
Emil Kolb Pkwy
Hwy 50
Humber
Bolton
Tract
Glasgow
Rd
Columbia Way
1 Cathedral Grove 130-ye
old hemlock forest
2 Young forest on slope
with old "wolf trees"
3 Old-growth forest on
the Humber floodplain
4 Old hemlock and dyin
ash forest.
0
0.5
1

By bike – The Caledon Trailway bike path could be used to access the Humber Valley Heritage Trail west of Bolton.

✤ What to do

This is a nice walk in the fall when colours are changing and the days are a little cooler (this trail has less shade than many in this book). It's an out-and-back hike unless you can arrange a pickup, and almost any length of time is worthwhile.

✤ Learn more

When I was a university student in the 1990s, my soil science professor showed us maps of the best soils in Canada (class 1 farmland), much of it in southern Ontario, with projections of urban growth. His message was clear: we were building on top of, and destroying, one of our most precious resources.

More than half of Canada's best farmland is found in Ontario, where urban development pressure is highest. And in fact, between 1971 and 2011, Canada lost nearly 4 million hectares of farmland mostly to urbanization—an area roughly the size of Vancouver Island. At the same time, markets for locally produced food are also enormous in southern Ontario.

One function of Ontario's Greenbelt is directly protecting farmland (protected countryside in the Greenbelt Plan includes the natural system, agricultural system, and settlement areas); there's also a fund that invests in local food initiatives. A 2015 report concluded that the Greenbelt does a great job protecting farmland, but prospects for farmland outside the Greenbelt are uncertain at best. The report states that, outside the Greenbelt "the land-use planning system in Ontario is geared toward the accommodation of urban (residential) development. Farmland is typically viewed as a background landscape upon which development is to be painted, or in other words, as tarmac-in-waiting."

The Humber Valley Trail winds between forest and farm fields

Under Doug Ford's Conservative government, things have certainly gotten worse: in 2021, Ontario lost an average of 319 acres of farmland per day, and the Ford government has been changing or overriding provincial land-use planning policies to prioritize low-density housing over agricultural and natural lands.

Even so, when I hike along the edge of farm fields protected by the Greenbelt in the Humber Valley, I'm grateful that my soil science teacher was at least partly wrong.

The trail begins in a small field off Glasgow Road, which was the site of an historic sawmill, built here in 1855. Today it is an old field starting to return to forest. At the far edge of the clearing is a grove of black

locust trees, some quite large—another testament to historical settlement in the area. This tree is native to a small area in the Appalachians and Ozark mountains of the United States but was often planted around old homesteads. Black locust is usually considered invasive in Canada, but it doesn't typically spread widely. This is in large part because it's native to North America, and when it spread from the southern US, it brought its own biocontrol with it. The locust borer is an insect pest that can stress and kill black locust trees. The adult can be recognized by its bee-like mimic pattern, and its habit of feeding on the pollen of goldenrod. Because goldenrod is ubiquitous in North America, the locust borer followed the tree as we planted it in many urban areas and around old homesteads. This

An adult locust borer feeding on the pollen of goldenrod

helped maintain a natural balance between the tree and its environment. In other parts of the world where the borer isn't present, black locust can be a more problematic invasive species. I'm not sure if in Canada black locust even is an invasive species; the term is usually defined as an introduced species that causes ecological or economic harm. It's not always obvious where that line should be drawn, but I'm not sure that black locust has crossed it. On the other hand, there are those who say there's no such thing as an invasive species, and to them I would say: how about emerald ash borer, a species that kills virtually every ash tree it encounters? There are countless examples of introduced species that cause enormous ecological and economic damage, as well as many other species, like dandelions, that are basically harmless, and a small grey area in the middle where species like black locust land. You can read about solutions to invasive species in the Thornton Bales Conservation Area, page 250.

Stay to the right at the black locust grove and cross the small footbridge over the Humber. The trail continues on the far side, leading past some old

Open grown "wolf trees" are valuable for wildlife, and they're beautiful.

Cathedral Grove on the Humber Valley Heritage Trail.

pear and apple trees, then eventually entering a mixed forest with black cherry and hemlock trees that has been dubbed "cathedral grove." It's a pretty hemlock forest, and the older trees from here to beyond the bend in the river reach at least 120-to 130-years, just entering the old-growth stage. As the trail climbs, there are even older forests along the increasingly steep slope, dominated by sugar maple and some hemlock. The views into the forest on the slopes of the Humber are delightful, especially in autumn. The forest was probably logged in the mid-1800s, but largely left alone ever since. The old forest continues on the slope to the left of the trail, until it descends a metal staircase through cedar and hemlock forest that is 130-to 140-years-old.

As you climb back out of the valley, you'll walk through a young sugar maple forest, but scattered throughout are huge, weirdly alien trees, with big knobbly branches and holes in the trunks. These are "wolf trees" that probably stood for a century or more in open pasture, providing welcome shade where grazing animals would congregate on hot days. In 1852, naturalist Henry David Thoreau described a pasture "with two or three great white oaks to shade the cattle, which the farmer would not take fifty dollars apiece for, though the shipbuilder wanted them." These lone sentinel trees, devoid of competition, rarely grow very tall, but instead spread their huge branches wide. They cast a lot of shade and also develop character unique to each tree. If the pasture is abandoned and the young forest finally overtakes them, these trees only get weirder as they struggle to grow taller and shed some of their lower branches, resulting in gnarly, twisted trunks and many bizarre growth forms. Sometimes wolf trees also grew along fencerows, their branches reaching far out in one direction where there was a field, while having clean branchless trunks on the side where there was forest. A lot of history is written into a wolf tree.

For many years, wolf trees were considered enemies of good forestry and were often cut down, but now they are increasingly appreciated, not only for their strange beauty and past service, but also for their value to wildlife. They are usually the oldest trees in the forests where they grow, and hollows created when they shed some of their massive branches provide home for many species of birds and mammals. In a 2011 article, biologist Michael Gaige describes spotting three times as many bird species in wolf trees as in surrounding mature trees. Birds such as scarlet tanagers, brown creepers, white-breasted nuthatches, black-capped chickadees, red-eyed vireos, and eastern wood pewees preferred the trees for foraging, singing, and occasionally nesting. Another time, he describes watching a coyote bolt from a hollow oak tree, adding, "I stuck my head inside to find six newborn pups wobbling around." The wolf trees are old-growth trees in a young forest, Gaige says, and wildlife respond to this. He is one of many people now singing the praises of wolf trees, a call that may be familiar to UK tree enthusiasts who have long honoured ancient "veteran" trees that stood alone for centuries on that landscape. A chimeric product of farm and forest, wolf trees are among the stars of the Humber Valley, and you may want to take a few minutes to appreciate the more fantastical specimens.

About midway between Emil Kolb parkway and Castlederg Side Road, the trail descends into the valley and another pocket of mature forest; the older trees are again probably 150-years-old or so, mostly sugar maple, but beginning with a nice white pine that greets you back to the old forest. Old white pines are rare in most forests because the wood was in great demand throughout the 19th and early 20th centuries. There are also a few old hemlocks growing downslope from the pine, and a lovely basswood in the valley. The forest in the valley is mixed; some of it was probably once lightly pastured; a section of barbed wire fence can be seen growing through a middle-aged maple, while the rest of the fence has probably rusted away under the lush green cover of ostrich and sensitive ferns.

Old-growth forest in the valley along the Humber Valley Trail.

One of the best examples of old forest occurs on the other side (NW) of Castlederg Side Road. The trail leads past old-growth hemlocks, mixed with younger yellow birch trees. The hemlocks are commonly 150-to 200-years-old, but some have characteristics suggesting they may be over 250-years-old. There are countless ash logs cut for trail safety. Ring counts from some of these tell us the ash trees reached at least 130-years-old before succumbing to emerald ash borer (learn more about invasive pests at Thornton Bales page 250).

Boyd Conservation Park and the Kortright Centre

✣ What you'll like

This very large diverse natural area is very accessible by car, and includes forest up to 200-years-old on the Berton Trail. The mix of trails offers the choice of a short hike and picnic, or a long day hike through multiple parks and habitats. You can walk parts of the original Carrying Place Trail. Excellent multi-use trails also help bring these parks closer together.

✣ How to get there

By car – Take the Islington Ave exit from the 401 (or Pine Valley exit from the 407) and follow Islington north to the park entrance. Or start at the Boyd North Parking Lot off Rutherford Road.

By public transit – Boyd Park can be reached in an hour and a half from Union Station. Take the subway to either Vaughan Metropolitan Centre (orange line terminus) or Pioneer Village stop, and take a combination of buses from there. Alternately, it's a reasonable bike ride from Vaughan Metropolitan Centre to various access points for Boyd Park. During hours when bikes are permitted on the subway, the combined trip should be a little faster than catching a bus (see below).

By bike – Boyd Park can be reached by bike within a couple of hours from many parts of Toronto, but it may include busy roads. The Humber River Recreation Trail offers a beautiful trail that can be followed for many kilometres, but the northern part of the route includes a long stretch on Islington Ave, until you can pick up the William Granger Greenway Trail. Alternately, you can bring your bike on the subway during off-peak hours or weekends and bike from Vaughan Metropolitan Centre, the final stop on the orange line. You can reach trailheads on Pine Valley or Islington in 25 minutes.

Part of the original Carrying Place trail may run along the Pine Valley road allowance at the edge of Boyd Park.

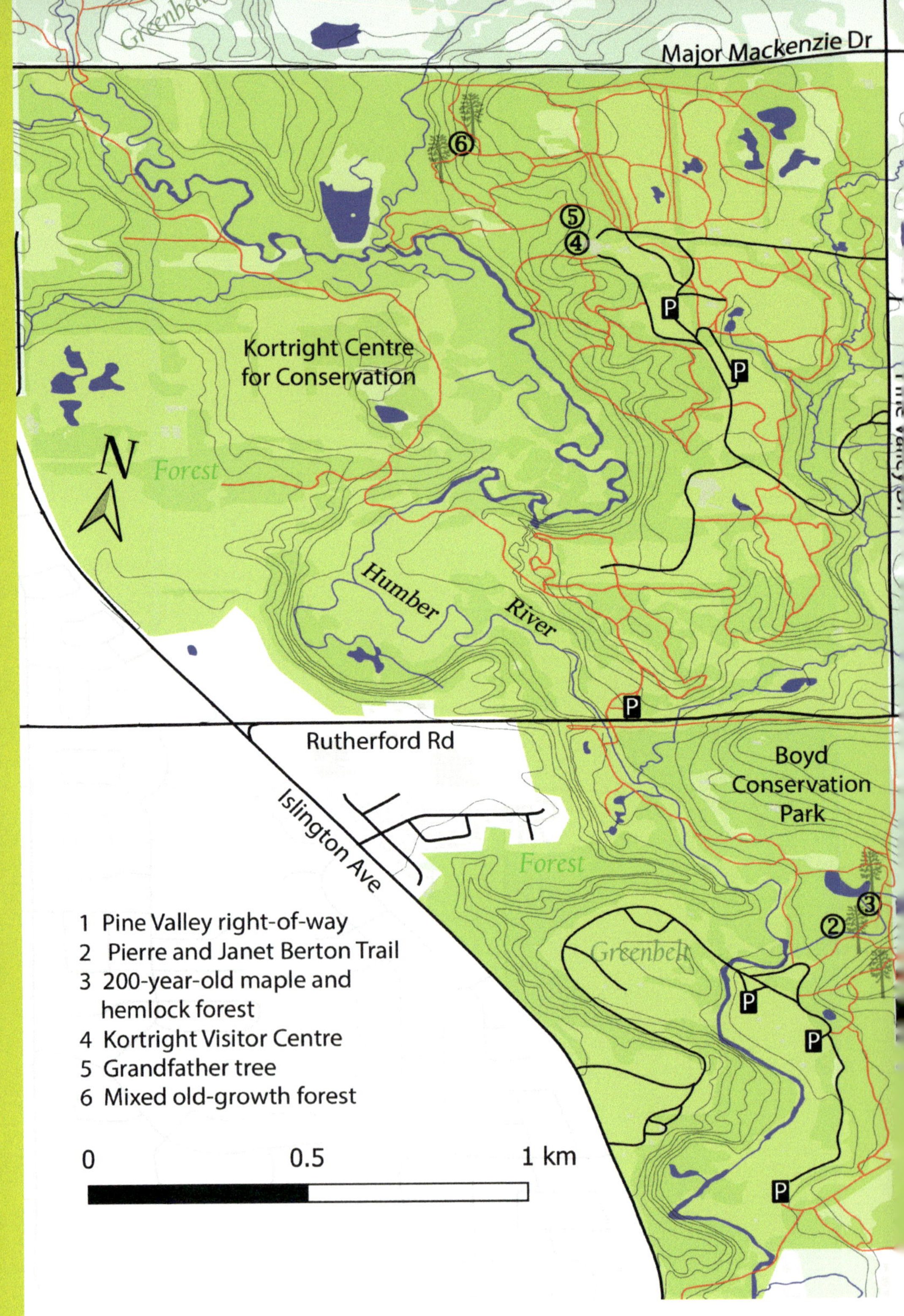

Major Mackenzie Dr
Kortright Centre
for Conservation
Forest
N
Humber
River
Rutherford Rd
Islington Ave
Boyd
Conservation
Park
Forest
Greenbelt
P
1 Pine Valley right-of-way
2 Pierre and Janet Berton Trail
3 200-year-old maple and
hemlock forest
4 Kortright Visitor Centre
5 Grandfather tree
6 Mixed old-growth forest
0
0.5
1 km

✤ What to do

You should plan to hike the Berton Trail. While there, you may want to find the side trail to the south end of the Pine Valley road allowance, where you can walk a short section of the Carrying Place Trail (or as close as you're likely to get to it). From the Berton trailhead, you'll be within reach of many other day hikes in Boyd, Kortright, and Glassco Parks. A bike can help bring some of the nature trails closer together. The McMichael Gallery is also worthwhile and can be reached on the multi-use trails in 20 minutes by bike, or an hour and a quarter on foot. Bring food and drink; there are some restaurants (mostly chains) in surrounding neighbourhoods, including a limited selection in Kleinburg at the end of the William Granger Greenway.

✤ Learn more

At Boyd Conservation Park we rejoin the route of the Toronto Carrying Place. In fact, the Carrying Place is said to have split at this point, with the two arms embracing Boyd Park and rejoining north of Kleinburg. A lot of Boyd Park is lowlands around the Humber River and the adjacent steep slopes, and it became a park after Hurricane Hazel made clear the folly of building on floodplains. Likewise, the Carrying Place tended to aim for the high ground to avoid seasonal flooding and dense thickets often found in valley bottoms, as well as steep climbs in and out of the valley.

Because of this, there may be places where modern roads or trails exactly follow the Carrying Place. One such place is Riverside Drive at the very start of the ancient route; another might be parts of the Pine Valley unopened road allowance. In his entertaining travelogue, Glenn Turner describes his walk away from Pine Valley onto TRCA lands, at the south end of the road allowance. "The deeper I penetrate into the wood, the more I become convinced that the Carrying Place must have looked very much

Bark balding is a sign of old age on this sugar maple along the Berton trail.

like this. In fact, not only is the look right, but the trail is just about in exactly the right location."

Turner tells us that the remains of a Wendat village were found nearby in Boyd Park, dating back to half a millennium ago when the Carrying Place was still an important travel route. Then, as now, communities flourished along travel routes and waterways. I'm happy to believe I'm following the route of the ancient trail. Initially the path follows a deep trough, then climbs to the ridge, while other trail branches drop into the valley. The Carrying Place would have taken the high route, which now dead ends at some homes (a lovely place to live, though I hope for the sake of the surrounding forest, they landscape with native plants). The other trails descend to meet up with the Pierre and Janet Berton Nature Trail.

The Berton trail runs through some of the nicest old-growth forest in Boyd Park, which also continues up the slope and across the Pine Valley road allowance, and is collectively called the Pine Valley Forest. It was recognized in the early 1980s as provincially significant for its mature forests and wetlands, with 30 vegetation communities on an area of 57 hectares. Nevertheless, by the late 1990s the plan was to build an 800-metre four-lane road to connect the orphaned ends of Pine Valley Drive, cutting through the heart of Pine Valley Forest.

Friends of Boyd Park organized a grassroots opposition to the road expansion, and got a boost from author and historian Pierre Berton. It's fitting that the renowned narrator of Canadian history would step in to help preserve one of the remnants of the Carrying Place Trail—as well as an old-growth forest where, it turns out, the Berton family used to picnic and winter camp. The extension was defeated, and in 2011 Patsy Berton, one of the family's eight children, attended the naming ceremony for the trail that commemorates both the Bertons and the fight to preserve the forest. "That place was near and dear to my parents' heart. It was a great community triumph," Berton told a reporter for the Newmarket Era at the ceremony. She said going back to the forest of her youth gave her chills, that it felt like a cathedral.

Some of the trees are probably over 200-years-old, suggesting that while this forest was likely logged, it was never completely cleared. There are hemlocks mixed with hardwoods and cedars in the valley, where the trail skirts the edge of wetlands. The maple–hemlock forest marches up the slopes and ravines. Reports from the 1980s show the significant old-growth forest crossing out of Boyd Conservation Area and continuing up the ravines, surrounded by suburban development. It's wild and untrailed; even the mountain bikers haven't found these parts of it (hikers should also stay away from this area of steep erosion-prone slopes, though snowshoers might try it in the depths of winter). This is the area that would have been sliced in half by the Pine Valley extension.

Next stop is the Kortright Centre, where naturalist and author James Garratt shows me around. Garratt's books are about the natural areas of the Greenbelt that he loves, and has helped fight to preserve, including the Rouge Valley and Glassco nature reserve where he lives, just north of Boyd Park. His books read like disjointed love letters to the land, but also sometimes like eulogies. He enumerates the species that he used to see and hear that have vanished over the decades: leopard frog, woodcock, eastern newt ... gone perhaps for good? But not forgotten by Garratt. Such is the cost of urbanization, and often we don't even know the exact causes. Noise, toxins, pets, edge-effects, drained wetlands, light pollution.

Speaking of light pollution, did you know that the largest optical telescope in Canada is in Richmond Hill? When the David Dunlap Observatory was built in 1935, Richmond Hill was basically in a dark sky preserve, far from urbanization. The observatory was in use and making important discoveries until the 1960s, when the city started to spread

Patsy Berton describes the Pine Valley Forest as feeling "like a cathedral."

around it and obscure the night sky with its glow. Now it is little more than a heritage site where the public can learn about astronomy. Many of us have had the experience of leaving the city and remembering that the night stars number not in the dozens we're used to seeing, but in the thousands; a magical display that can still take my breath away all these years later.

We don't have to give up as much of the night as we think. Consider Sherbrooke, Quebec, a city of 167,000 people where the LED streetlights are a warm amber colour and the night sky is far more visible. Light on the amber end of the spectrum not only scatters less, letting the stars shine through, it also affects sleep less and is far better for insects and wildlife, improving urban biodiversity. And visibility is actually better under amber LEDs because there is less glare and scattering of the light. An easy change to make to improve our quality of life, while preserving urban biodiversity. I digress.

It's the cumulative multi-faceted impacts of urbanization that make the Greenbelt valuable when compared to a patchwork of isolated parks in a sea of sprawl. Consider Boyd Park, which connects to Kortright and Glassco Nature Reserve (over 700 hectares total), as well as a ribbon of green along the Humber River to the south, and then the whole of the Greenbelt to the north. Garratt shows me some old forest in Boyd, not quite as old as the Berton trail but worth visiting. And he shows me the well-worn trail he follows to work each day, walking from Glassco Park to the Kortright Centre. I work hard to keep up as he walks quickly and confidently on the uneven trails of Boyd, but I imagine moments when he pauses on his daily walk, such as he describes in his book *Nature Reserve on the City's Edge*: "Time stands still [...] You're alone with the morning. Green light is in the cedars, along with tints of robin's-egg blue, cardinal red. The moment pivots, turning with the sun."

Also to the north, nestled within Glassco Park and the Greenbelt, is the McMichael Canadian Art Collection, which houses exclusively Canadian art—including the Group of Seven, Emily Carr, Norval Morrisseau, Doris McCarthy, and other Canadian painters who capture the essence of the land. Consider that the east branch of the Carrying Place trail would have run steps away from the gallery, also the association with Pierre Berton and the pockets of centuries-old forest in Boyd Park, and you can't help but feel humbled by the sweep of Canadian culture, landscape, and history dating back thousands of years.

James Garrat crossing a small bridge that is part of his daily commute.

Maple Nature Reserve

✣ What you'll like

The old forest, swamp, and river valley offer a shady oasis that contrasts with the open plantation forest on the ridge. The combination makes for a diverse, interesting hike. Some of the more unusual trees in the arboretum plantation might catch the attention of tree nerds. This forest could be combined with others in the area in a daytrip.

✣ How to get there

By car – This forest is easily accessed from the 401 or 407 via Allen Road and Dufferin Street. From the 400, follow Major Mackenzie Drive. Parking is at 10401 Dufferin Street, or off Teston Road.

By public transit – You can reach the nature reserve in 1 to 2 hours from Union Station, depending on the schedule. The fastest way to get there is to catch the GO train toward Barrie and get off at Maple Station (about 35 minutes from Union, or 15 minutes from Downsview Park). From Maple Station, you can catch a bus along Major Mackenzie, or simply walk about half an hour to the Nature Reserve.

By bike – Maple Nature Reserve is about 25 minutes by bike from Richmond Hill GO station, and 10 minutes from Maple GO station. Bike ON and Ontario Bike Route routes run through Aurora (Wellington Street) about 45 minutes to the north.

✣ What to do

If you live nearby, consider visiting on wet spring nights to watch for migrating salamanders. Maple Nature Reserve offers relatively short trails, and you may wish to combine it with a visit to Boyd Park, or Sugarbush Heritage Park (Baker's Woods) in Thornhill. The latter isn't

The short Salamander Trail is one of the best places to visit the old-growth forest in Maple Nature Reserve.

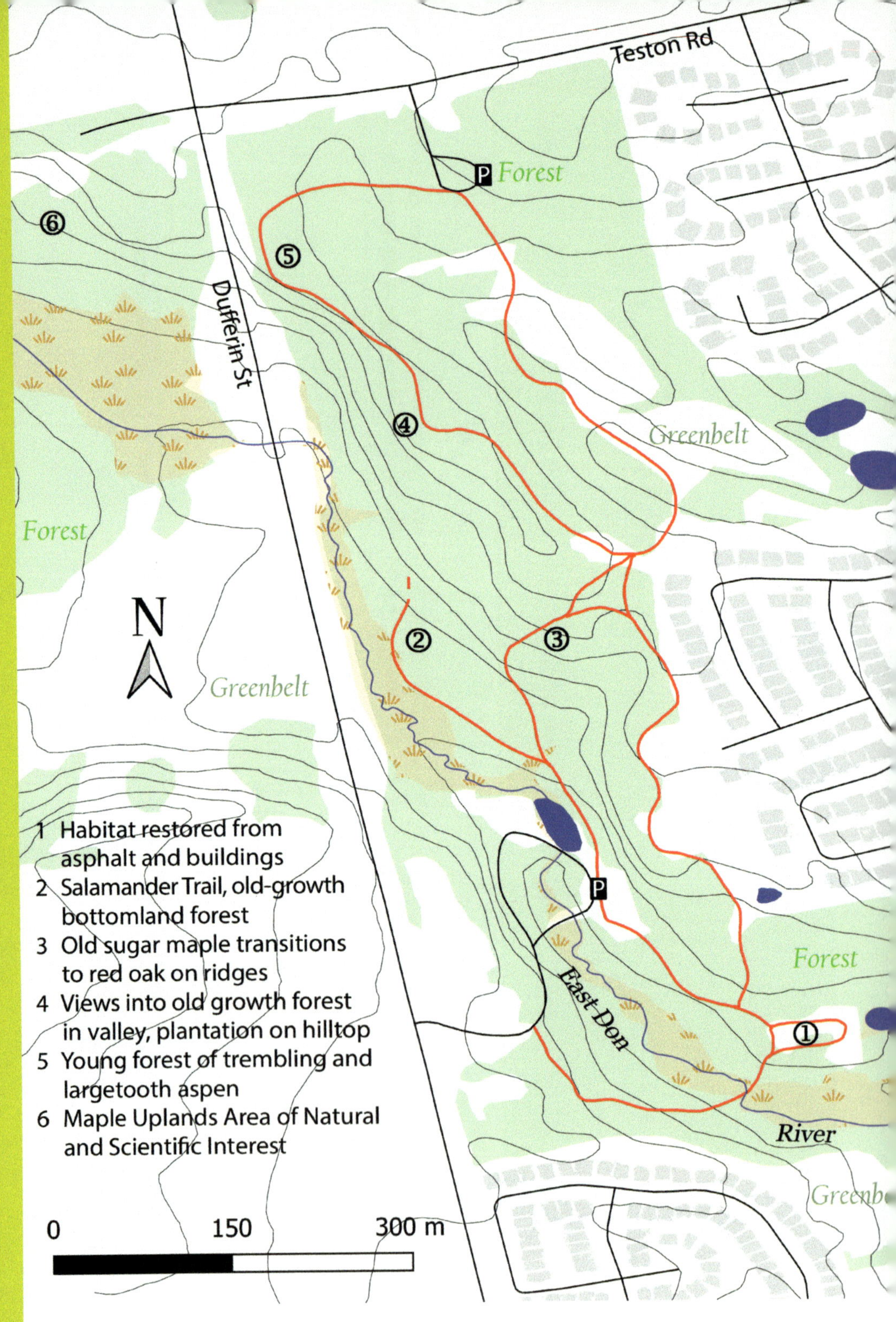

Teston Rd
Forest
Dufferin St
Greenbelt
Forest
N
Greenbelt
Forest
East Don
River
Greenb
1 Habitat restored from asphalt and buildings
2 Salamander Trail, old-growth bottomland forest
3 Old sugar maple transitions to red oak on ridges
4 Views into old growth forest in valley, plantation on hilltop
5 Young forest of trembling and largetooth aspen
6 Maple Uplands Area of Natural and Scientific Interest
0
150
300 m

included in this book, mostly because it is outside the Greenbelt, but it has many old sugar maple trees from over a century of being managed as a sugar bush and is close by.

✣ Learn more

This small, quirky little nature reserve is part of a larger natural area that extends across Dufferin Street and further north. It is on a spur of the Oak Ridges Moraine that juts to the south, and ground water seepages feed into the headwaters of the East Don River. The East Don Valley is particularly broad with extensive bottomlands shaped by glacial meltwater thousands of years ago. The spring-fed wetlands and vernal (temporary) pools that form in the valley bottom are breeding habitat for various amphibians, including species rarely found in urban areas such as wood frog, northern leopard frog, and spotted salamander.

Most amphibians need small pools without fish in which to lay their eggs and start a new generation of tadpoles and efts. Sometime before the end of the summer (depending on the species) they grow legs and walk out of the pool to become adults. Old-growth forests can provide superior breeding habitat because when large old-growth trees are blown over in a windstorm, the roots mat tips up, bringing a large amount of soil with it. The resulting pit and mound can persist for many centuries in most forest soils, outlasting any trace of the tree that caused them. In low-lying areas, the pits fill with spring rain and melt water long enough for a generation of frogs and salamanders to emerge. Large logs from the fallen trees can also last hundreds of years, providing a moist habitat that most salamander species love to live in or under. So, an old-growth forest really is a salamander forest, and they can be amazingly abundant. In very rich habitats, there may be as many as one salamander for every square metre!

Old-growth forest at Maple Nature Reserve.

Frogs announce their presence to the world each spring with croaks, chuckles, rattles, and peeps of the strangest variety, but salamanders are in permanent stealth mode. Mostly living underground or beneath leaf litter or rotting logs, they are hardly ever seen except during mating season, when during early spring they travel at night to lay eggs in small pools of water, before vanishing again for another year. The most cryptic of all are spotted salamanders, which are so reclusive they don't even meet up to mate. Male spotted salamanders simply wander around a promising pool, leaving sperm packets for the female to collect and use to fertilize her eggs. The eggs are bright green because they have symbiotic algae in them that photosynthesize, providing energy and oxygen (important in the stagnant oxygen-poor pools where they are laid). In fact, we now know that the larvae themselves have algae within their cells, making them the only vertebrate species that is known to photosynthesize! Once the adults emerge from the pools, you're very unlikely to ever see one except perhaps a few wet nights in the early spring. They live in burrows or under rocks or logs, eating insects, worms, and spiders, living for several decades and growing to 15 (or even 25!) cm long.

So now you know where the Salamander Trail gets its name. This short dead-end trail is also a good place to get a look at the old-growth forest on the valley bottom and ravine slopes, while the longer upland trail loop offers some views into the valley from above. Trees reach at least 180-years-old and probably more, predominantly hemlock in the valley, sugar maple on the slopes, and some red oaks near the ridge. The small loop to the south goes by some nice largish red oaks, scattered hemlocks, and a small pond with a lot of cup plant growing around it.

The numerous trails in Maple Nature Reserve set it apart from a large natural area on the west side of Dufferin Street, which is inaccessible. Trails have impacts that range from trampling of native plants to flushing

A hemlock branch in autumn is decorated with red maple leaves like a Christmas tree.

birds. Several sensitive ground-nesting birds such as ovenbird, veery, and woodcock are found to the west of Dufferin, but are absent from Maple Nature Reserve. People walking in the area can flush birds from the nests or disturb feeding, but dogs are a bigger culprit. A 2007 study showed that dog walking in forests causes losses of 35% in bird diversity, and 41% in abundance, with even higher impacts on ground-nesting birds. Never let your dog off leash in large forest areas. Even if dogs are permitted on leash, you probably shouldn't bring them to some of the more natural forests during breeding season in spring and early summer.

Of course, trails serve the function of connecting people to the forest, which is essential for long-term conservation, not to mention human health and wellbeing. It's especially important to get kids out in nature, for all kinds of reasons. But I'm glad there's also a large trail-less area to the west where many forest interior birds are thriving that are found rarely in Maple Nature Reserve. By being careful with how and when we use the trails, we can also reduce our impact, and maybe allow some wildlife to return.

Maple Nature Reserve was home to a Department of Lands and Forests and Ministry of Natural Resources research station from the 1950s to the 1990s. Experimental plantations, mostly of conifers and hybrid poplars, are still seen on the ridge in the northeast part of the nature reserve. There are also many invasive plant species growing among the tree varieties, especially Asian bittersweet (a climbing vine that can strangle trees) and dog-strangling vine.

Eaton Hall (Seneca College, King Campus)

✣ What you'll like

The Oak Ridges Trail runs past Eaton Hall, through old-growth forests, over spring-fed streams, and around Lake Seneca to reach Marylake, the one-time estate of Sir Henry Pellatt. Pellatt was an infamous financier in the early 20th century who built Casa Loma, now a Toronto tourist attraction. This is a beautiful part of the Oak Ridges Trail that leads past several types of old-growth forest, the Eaton Hall mansion, and the Marylake monastery, with impressive brick barns of the Pellatt estate.

✣ How to get there

By car – Paid parking is available at the campus. A parking lot next to the sugarbush or parking near Eaton Hall offer good parking options.

By public transit – King Campus of Seneca College is easily reached by public transit from King city via YRT Bus #22 and other routes. Use the York Region Transit website (yrt.ca) to plan your trip.

By bike – An Ontario Bike Route runs through Aurora (Wellington Street) 13 minutes to the north.

✣ What to do

You can either park beside the sugar bush or continue on to park at Eaton Hall (both are paid parking). The short loop at the sugarbush won't take long to walk. From there, follow the trail along the lake, past Eaton Hall and into the adjacent old growth, continuing as far as you like before turning around. From Eaton Hall you can make a partial loop through younger woods and fields. All of this can be done in a couple of hours. If you have a little longer, continuing along the Oak Ridges Trail to Marylake is worthwhile, mostly for Henry Pellatt's brick barns.

Sir Henry Pellatt signs the guest book on a visit to Casa Loma in 1937. City of Toronto Archives, Fonds 1244, Item 4013.

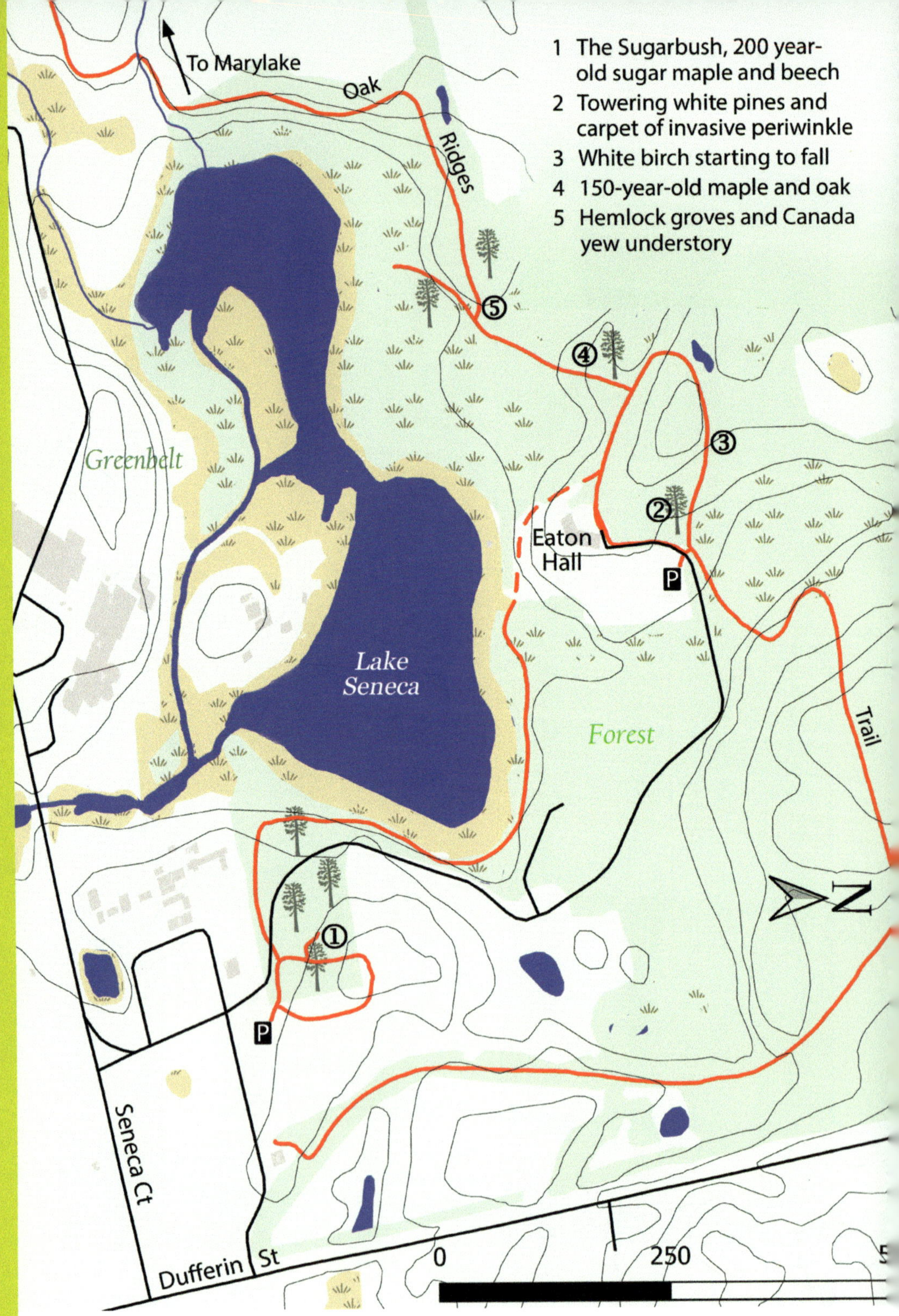
1 The Sugarbush, 200 year-old sugar maple and beech
2 Towering white pines and carpet of invasive periwinkle
3 White birch starting to fall
4 150-year-old maple and oak
5 Hemlock groves and Canada yew understory
To Marylake
Oak Ridges
Greenbelt
Lake Seneca
Eaton Hall
Forest
Trail
N
Seneca Ct
Dufferin St
0
250

✣ Learn more

In the early 1900s, John Craig (Jack) Eaton was vice president and heir to the Eaton department stores, and he and his wife, Flora, were near the pinnacle of the Toronto elite. One evening around a century ago, they were entertaining their good friend, Annie Dobie, in the music room of their mansion in Toronto. Their neighbour, Sir Henry Pellatt, who was living in the unfinished Casa Loma, rang at the door and Mr. Eaton left to speak with him.

"Presently the two men joined us, laughing heartily," Flora Eaton describes in her memoir. She asked what the joke was, and Sir Henry replied, "I told Jack I knew of a beautiful farm near Lake Marie which he should buy. He said he didn't want a farm, so I told him to go to hell, and I'd come talk to you, as you know something about farms." Their friend, Mrs. Dobie, chimed in, "You know good neighbours when you have them! You want them in the country as well as in town." "You're right," Sir Henry declared.

The charismatic Sir Henry prevailed and, in the winter of 1920, he and the Eatons journeyed together in a private rail car to a siding at Pellatt's farm. From there they took a sleigh to see the farm that the Eatons would then buy. Lady Eaton would eventually build Eaton Hall on the property after her husband's untimely death.

You retrace part of this sleigh ride as you walk the Oak Ridges Trail from Eaton Hall to Marylake—the old railway siding has now been coopted to be part of the trail. And while most of the old-growth forest is found near Eaton Hall, the huge brick barn of Pellatt's former estate (at the time, and probably still, the largest brick barn in Canada) is also a notable attraction.

Pellatt was a larger than life character who built larger than life things, but none of his plans was ever completed. The grand country house he envisioned at Lake Marie was never built. Only 23 rooms of the 98 at Casa Loma were ever fully finished. And Sir Henry, who had been counted

Sir Henry Pellatt built the largest brick barn in Canada on his country estate, now the Marylake Augustinian Monastery.

among the wealthiest of Canadians, ended up destitute and living with his chauffeur by the time he died. He was unable to pay for the upkeep of Casa Loma, which became a hotel for a time, then sat empty until the City of Toronto took it in 1933 in exchange for $27,305.45 in unpaid taxes.

Sir Henry visited the famous house one more time in 1937, when he was invited to speak to the Kiwanis club, which was running Casa Loma as a tourist attraction. In a touching scene, he rose to speak as the crowd began singing "Old Soldiers Never Die." Pellatt had to cover his face with his hands for a few moments to hide his tears, then he repeated the first lines of the song: "Old soldiers never die, they just fade away." He went on to say, "I am delighted to be here, and I am sorry that it has affected me so. I built Casa Loma principally as a place where people would enjoy themselves. Your club is now using it for that purpose and bringing enjoyment and happiness to countless people. It could not be put to better use. I am satisfied."

The Lake Marie estate was sold in 1935 and became the Marylake Augustinian Monastery. Pellatt moved into an apartment in Toronto. By the time he died in 1939, he had $185 in cash but owed over $6000. The construction of Eaton Hall was completed in the same year, and Lady Eaton lived in it until her death in 1970, when it was sold to Seneca College. Shortly after she moved into Eaton Hall, the Second World War broke out, and children and families from Britain were invited to shelter in the grand home during the war. "So, suddenly, my household expanded, and rooms and gardens were full of the laughter and squabbles of youngsters," she wrote in her autobiography, *Memory's Wall*. She also wrote about the many Christmases hosted in the house, which was filled with singing, feasting, and toasts. Looking up at the windows of Eaton Hall, I can't help imagining her looking out from one of them in her later years, pausing from her writing to reflect on days past.

Under the ownership of the wealthy Eaton family, the mature forests around Seneca Lake were left alone to grow into the old-growth forests we see today. "Eaton Hall grounds are mostly as nature left them," Lady Eaton wrote in her memoir, adding, "Throughout the acres of natural woodland we continue to plant bulbs and other plants to give colour every springtime." Many of those plants have long since faded away, but a few remain. Periwinkle is one of them, and it has slowly crept over the entire hillside near the house, crowding out ferns and other native plants under the towering old-growth

Invasive periwinkle has spread to cover hectares of land near Eaton Hall.

white pines and sugar maples. Periwinkle is a creeping ground cover that spreads so slowly you might be pardoned for thinking it isn't invading at all. But over the decades, periwinkle and Lily of the Valley have covered acres of land, their spread only (mostly) stopped by the laneway that formerly led to Eaton Hall—now part of the Oak Ridges Trail. It serves as a warning of the insidious, relentless nature of invasive species.

Periwinkle is still widely sold in nurseries despite being a highly invasive plant. Just because a plant is for sale at a nursery doesn't mean it isn't harmful! Fortunately, it has never been easier to buy a wide variety of native plants. One of my simplest and most enduring pleasures is learning about native plants and growing them in my yard, where they create food and habitat for many insect and bird species. Lorraine Johnson's books on native plant gardens are a great place to start learning, as is the North American Native Plant Society (nanps.org), which lists native plant nurseries. Also the plant list in the final pages of this book.

Despite the legacy of invasive garden plants, the land around Seneca Lake is an ecological gem. Located just south of the height of land on the Oak Ridges Moraine, ground water emerges in a number of seepages, along with small spring-fed streams that feed into Lake Seneca, one of several kettle lakes in the area. In the spring and early summer, you'll hear the piercing, ever louder call of the oven bird: tea-cher! tea-cher! tea-cher! Few birds announce their presence more stridently, and few are as secretive as they go about building their nests and raising their young. The oven bird's nest is just a hollow mound of leaves on the ground that blends perfectly into the surrounding leaf litter. Healthy populations of ground-nesting ovenbirds, winter wren, and northern waterthrush are a testament to the ecological health of the forests at King campus. All ground-nesting birds are particularly vulnerable to predation by cats and raccoons that thrive in urban areas, as well as disturbance by dogs.

There are several places to see old-growth forest at King Campus. Some of the oldest trees are found in a small patch of forest near the entrance to the campus, just east of Lake Seneca. This was probably an old sugar bush on the original farm. Many of the sugar maples show signs of old age, like bark balding, sinuous trunks, and large twisted branches high in the canopy, and likely reach at least 200-years-old. Most of the beech trees in the forest have died of beech bark disease. There's a small side trail to a particularly charismatic large sugar maple tree.

From the old sugar bush, you can cross the road and follow a trail near the shore of Lake Seneca, past more old trees, through thickets of shrubs, and finally across the lawn in front of Eaton Hall. Once you pass in front of Eaton Hall, you can rejoin the Oak Ridges Trail. Follow the laneway for a minute and watch for a smaller foot trail that climbs the ridge. On either side of the trail are sugar maples and red oaks that reach 150-years-old or more. After a while, the trail descends into wet forest of hemlock and cedar, where the trees are still quite old, though many are smaller. The extensive swamp forest at Eaton Hall is valuable habitat for amphibians like spring peepers, wood frogs, and grey tree frogs. Also, it hosts some plants that thrive in wet soils, such as alder-leaved buckthorn (our native buckthorn), three-leaved false Solomon's seal, and twinflower.

Continue to follow the Oak Ridges Trail and, if you like, you can follow a side trail to the left that parallels Keele Street and runs along the edge of some old forest—or cross Keele to Marylake Monastery, which was Sir Henry Pellatt's former estate almost a century ago. If you are visiting Marylake, the trail continues for a while after crossing Keele Street, then hits a T-intersection. Turn left here and watch for white blazes that lead past the barn and along the shore of the lake. This turn isn't clearly marked, though most of the rest of the trail is.

Thornton Bales Conservation Area

✣ What you'll like

Descending through the forest canopy on the "99 steps," you'll be impressed by the large red oak, ash, and maple trees, as well as a rich understory community of ferns, wild ginger, ground pine, and other plants. These are among the finest old-growth forests on the Oak Ridges Moraine, after Peter's Woods. It abuts University of Toronto's Jokers Hill, and the combined natural area offers extensive hiking trails through a variety of ecosystems, right at the edge of Newmarket.

✣ How to get there

By car – The closest parking is on 19th Sideroad (44.027, -79.519), though space can be limited on nice weekends. University of Toronto trails also access the old-growth forest, and it's a 40-minute hike from the Jokers Hill Trail Parking to Thornton Bales Conservation Area.

By public transit – York region transit Bus #57 takes you to the Joker Hill Trailhead off Bathurst Street (44.041, -79.504). It's a 15-minute bus ride or 35-minute walk from the Newmarket GO Bus station to the Jokers Hill trailhead.

By bike – This conservation area is on the Greenbelt Cycle Route, and a short ride from Newmarket.

✣ What to do

The Conservation Area access trail and loop are relatively short but beautiful. You may want to take some time to learn your ferns or other plants, have lunch, and enjoy the view from the 99 steps, and hug some trees along the edge of the trail. You can easily combine the loop trail with a longer hike at Jokers Hill or cycling on the Greenbelt Route. Walking

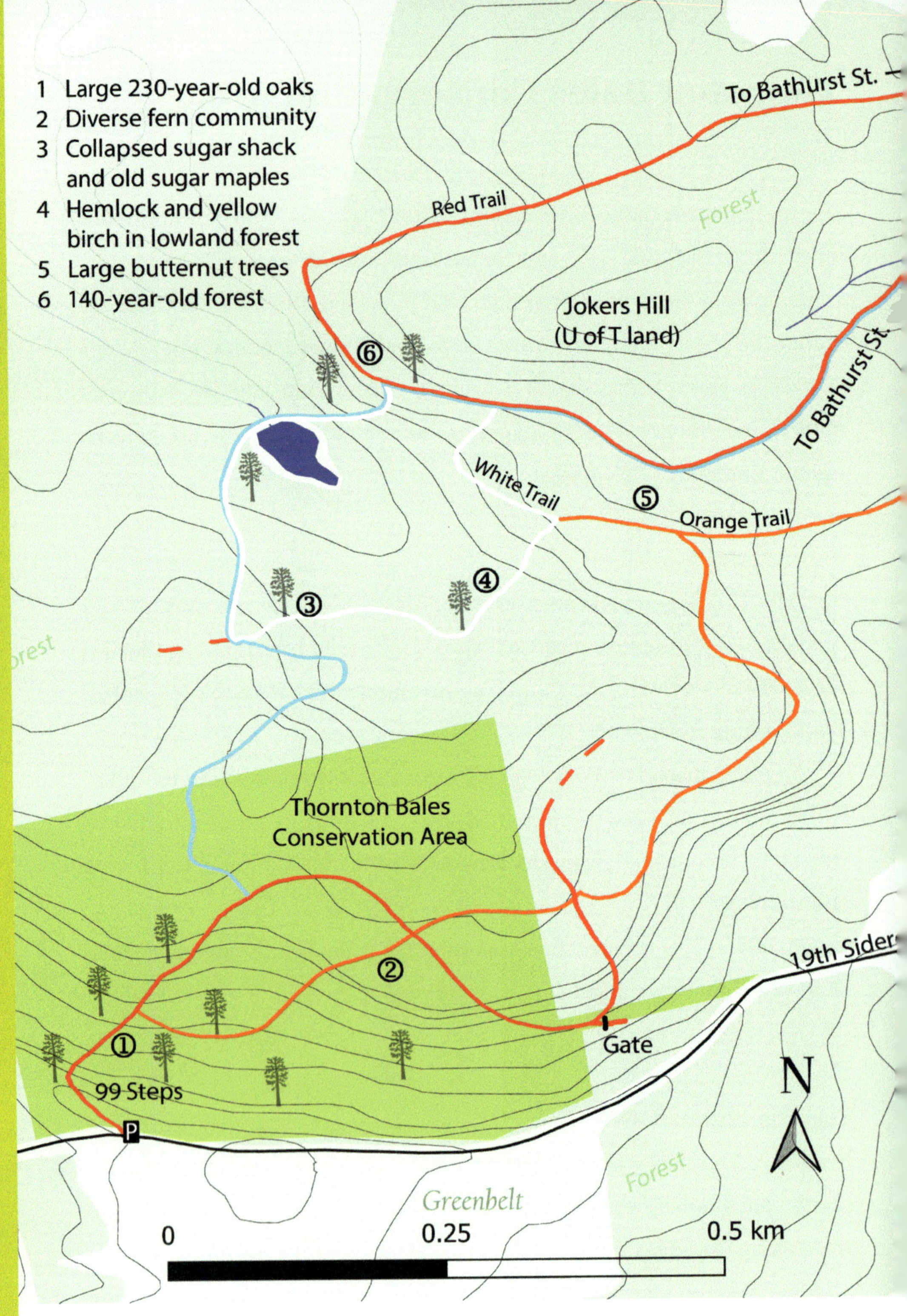
1 Large 230-year-old oaks
2 Diverse fern community
3 Collapsed sugar shack and old sugar maples
4 Hemlock and yellow birch in lowland forest
5 Large butternut trees
6 140-year-old forest
To Bathurst St.
Red Trail
Forest
Jokers Hill
(U of T land)
To Bathurst St.
White Trail
Orange Trail
Thornton Bales
Conservation Area
19th Sider
Gate
99 Steps
P
N
Forest
Greenbelt
0
0.25
0.5 km

from the Newmarket GO bus station, you could be at the old-growth forest in an hour and a quarter, much of it on the Jokers Hill trails, making it a feasible day trip by public transit from many parts of Toronto. It can get pretty busy; you may want to save this one for a weekday or out of peak season. It's beautiful when the leaves are opening in early May.

✣ Learn more

Thousands of years ago, a large section of the north slope of the Oak Ridges Moraine sloughed off in a massive landslide, just west of what is now Newmarket. No one knows why—it might have been caused by an earthquake, or by unstable soil saturated with water after heavy rains. The result today is a precipitous drop into Thornton Bales Conservation Area and impressive views into the forest when the leaves are on, or over the surrounding landscape when the trees are bare. More than thirty years ago, a campaign for the conservation of this beautiful forest included letter writing by naturalists and scientists, intervention by the Federation of Ontario Naturalists, and rogue tree spiking by an anonymous individual. Some of the 230-year-old oak trees growing on the slope may still have tree spikes buried within, but the campaign was only partly successful. Some of the forest was logged in the 1980s, but the oldest oaks were left alone.

Walking down the 99 steps into the Conservation Area, you're literally climbing down through the forest canopy, descending a height greater than the drop over Niagara Falls. The steep slopes and rolling hills are forested with old-growth sugar maple, beech, red oak, and white ash. Trees are commonly 100-to 200-years-old, and some of the oldest red oaks reach over 230 years. Throughout Thornton Bales, the relatively undisturbed forest has a rich understory, including abundant ferns and wild ginger, hobblebush and hairy honeysuckle. At the base of the slope, seepage coming off the Oak Ridges Moraine creates a wet forest on the

The “99 steps” descend from the Oak Ridges Moraine into Thornton Bales Conservation Area.

Lake Simcoe lowlands, where moisture-loving trees such as cedar, red maple, hemlock, and yellow birch are common. The seepage swamp forest on the lowlands is punctuated by many small hills that are actually glacial deposits called kames.

Kames form when depressions in glacial ice are filled with sediment deposited by glacial meltwater. Small glacial lakes and potholes are gradually filled in, and when the ice finally melts, everything's inverted and the lakes become hills (the same process that on a much vaster scale created the Moraine itself). Kames can be single hills, but more commonly they form a hummocky terrain, and may be associated with kettle lakes (as at Eaton Hall), which are created by the melting of large buried blocks of ice. Thornton Bales is extra special geologically because of the combination of kame topography and the very unusual landslide scar.

Thornton J. Bales bought the property in 1911, and rather than log it (as many landowners would have), he donated it to King Township to preserve it, which turned it over to the Lake Simcoe Region Conservation Authority in 1961. The site was identified in the early 1980s as an Area of Natural and Scientific Interest (ANSI), significant for both its unusual geology and its old-growth forests. It was also recognized as an environmentally significant area by the Lake Simcoe Region Conservation Authority. Almost immediately after designating it, foresters at the Conservation Authority started making a plan to log Thornton Bales, despite its designation as both an ANSI and ESA. Maybe this would have flown under the radar until it was too late, but it was surrounded by a University of Toronto research forest; graduate students in the university's botany department noticed the plan and started organizing. After a campaign of letter writing and lobbying by the students and the Federation of Ontario Naturalists in 1987–88, as a compromise, the site was logged but much less heavily than planned. Most of the oldest trees were left. It only takes one land manager or board of directors to log a property, while it takes generations of stewardship to preserve it. In this case it was a bit of each.

Even today many ANSIs in Ontario have little formal protection from logging, unless they have tax-exempt status, but the scales have tipped, and logging old-growth forest on public land in Southern Ontario is less publicly acceptable. A greater danger for most old-growth forests in Southern Ontario today is invasive species, especially introduced tree-killing insects and diseases.

When I walked down the 99 steps in 2019, I was welcomed to the forest by some big, beautiful ash trees. By the time you visit this forest, many or even all of these trees will have been killed by emerald ash borer, a pest introduced from Asia around the turn of the millennium that is killing most of the ash trees in North America. Last year a friend told me over a beer that he cries whenever he goes to a local natural area and walks among the dead and dying ash trees. I think this is an appropriate response. Consider that not only are ash trees dying, but their offspring will die, too, once they mature enough to be attacked by the borer. And it is not just one species but all North American species in the ash genus Fraxinus.

However, we aren't built to live in that place of sadness. I sometimes wonder if a lot of the denialism that accompanies environmental issues is just a way of dealing with loss, getting stuck in the first stage of grief. There are better ways to move on from the sadness, though, like finding hope and taking action.

In this case, consider that not every ash tree will die. Survival rates are very low—over 99% of ash trees usually die when an area is infested—but the rare trees that remain alive often carry resistance genes that helped them fend off the borer, and which can be passed on to their offspring. Old-growth forests have been shown to have high genetic diversity, so Thornton Bales might be a particularly good place to watch for resistance. Several species of

Christmas fern and wild ginger are part of the diverse understory plant community at Thornton Bales.

wasps introduced for biological control have also helped somewhat to keep emerald ash borer in check, offering another source of hope that ash trees might remain familiar to our children and grandchildren.

Until recently, the most notable tree in Thornton Bales was a butternut tree on the north side of the loop, close to a boardwalk and the junction with the Jokers Hill trails. This old-growth butternut tree died in 2020 from an introduced fungus called butternut canker. Many of the young butternut trees near the trails on the east side of the conservation area are diseased and dying, but a few large trees remain. Disease-resistant butternut trees are rare, but we know they exist. Just to confuse things, some seemingly resistant butternuts are actually hybrids with Japanese walnut trees.

Butternuts are graceful trees, and because of their very nutritious nuts, they were valuable to wildlife and culturally important. Indigenous North Americans ate the nuts, extracted oil from them, and used them for medicines and dyes. The wood is very soft, but rich amber in colour, and

This endangered butternut tree grew adjacent to the trail until it was recently killed by an introduced fungus.

it can catch the light and shimmer, an effect woodworkers called "flame." Butternut was once common enough to be used as a dye for Confederate Army uniforms in the American Civil War, but because of butternut canker it is now an endangered species.

It's tempting to blame the onslaught of tree-killing pests and diseases on climate change, but in fact it's the result of international trade. This brings us back to another alternative to despair: taking action. Accidental introduction of tree-killing pests and diseases is a relatively easy problem to fix; we just need the personal and political will to do it, and that's where you come in, through careful gardening and by voting or contacting your representatives.

International trade is killing our forests, but we can fix it

The list is long—Dutch elm disease, beech bark disease, emerald ash borer, butternut canker, hemlock woolly adelgid, and many more. On average, a new destructive insect pest or pathogen arrives in North America every 2 to three years. These tree killers have several things in common: they all come from other continents; they were accidentally introduced; they are killing our native trees; and they could have been stopped. In fact, the cost of stopping the insects and diseases before they arrive is much cheaper than dealing with the consequences after they arrive.

Wood boring insects are imported primarily in packaging materials—wood boxes or pallets—whereas pathogens and other pests mostly come over with live plants. There are measures in place to control each of these pathways of introduction, but they aren't enough to actually fix the problem. In fact, with increasing global trade, the problem is expected to get worse, not better.

Simple solutions have been proposed by the Cary Institute of Ecosystem Studies, based in Millbrook, New York, which is promoting a program called Tree-SMART trade. Though it originates in the United States, the policy solutions apply in Canada and many other countries. Implementation of Tree-SMART Trade would see us switch away from types of wood packaging capable of transporting pests, put greater restrictions on importation of some live plants, enforce penalties on non-compliant shipments, improve early detection and response programs, and work with trading partners to recognize problem species before they arrive in North America.

All of these measures will cost money in the short term, but save far more money within a couple of decades. The cost of managing emerald ash borer is expected to top half a billion dollars for Canadian municipalities alone, mostly for cutting and planting trees. Asian long-horned beetle, should it arrive, would have a devastating impact on maple syrup producers, small woodlot owners, tourism, etc.

Tackling this problem will also help fight climate change; a 2019 study found that the amount of carbon released each year as trees are killed by invasive pests is equivalent to the emissions of five million vehicles.

Given that inaction is ultimately more costly than action, it's unconscionable that we haven't done more to control tree-killing invasive species. Even if there were a net cost to action, many of us would happily pay it if we didn't have to watch swathes of trees continue to die, and tree species disappear from our forests.

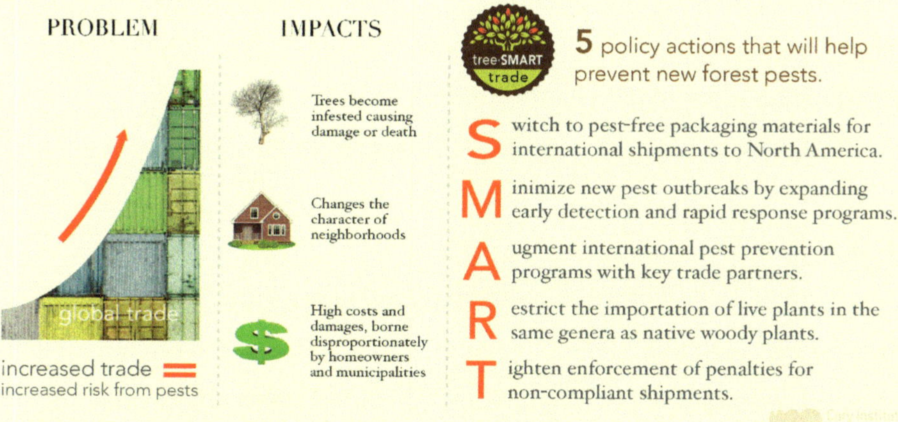

Hollidge Tract

✤ What you'll like

A pleasant walk through a diversity of forest types, including a nice hemlock swamp. Walk as far as you want on the Oak Ridges Trail and York Regional Forest trails. Most of the trails are relatively flat and easy, and usually not too busy.

✤ How to get there

By car – There is good roadside parking at the trailhead on Ninth Line (44.0708, -79.2786), or park at the Bill Fisch Forest Stewardship and Education Centre, and the accessible trail off Hwy 48.

By public transit – There is no convenient public transit. GO stations in Stouffville or Newmarket could be used as a launch point for bike or taxi/ride hailing.

By bike – The Greenbelt Cycle Route runs about three kilometres south on Ninth Line and Aurora Road. Hollidge Tract can be reached by bike from Stouffville GO in about 45 minutes, or an hour from Newmarket GO station.

✤ What to do

This is a good, relatively easy walk that can be done in a few hours or less. It can also be combined with hikes in other York Region forests, several of which are just west of Highway 48. Thornton Bales and Eaton Hall are also nearby.

✤ Learn more

This is the youngest forest in this book and one of the most historically disturbed, but in many ways it's also emblematic of the Greenbelt. You're greeted to the tract by an old red pine plantation that is transitioning into

The Hollidge Tract invites you in.

Hwy 48
Greenbelt
Vivian Rd
Forest
P
④
Hollidge
Tract
1 Plantation transitioning to natural forest
2 Old-growth cedar and hemlock forest; old pine stumps
3 Old maple forest
4 Bill Fisch Forest Stewardship and Education Centre
③
②
①
Oak Ridges Trail
Forest
St. John's Sideroad
Greenbelt
N
0
200
400 m

sugar maple forest. The existence of the Hollidge Tract, and the York Regional Forest, can be traced back to one individual, E.J. Zavitz, who arguably laid the groundwork for Ontario's Greenbelt nearly a century before its creation. Zavitz was part of a larger conservation movement of the time that sought to restore a damaged landscape left after the worst excesses of colonization.

Much of the Oak Ridges Moraine should never have been cleared for agriculture. After trees were cut (and often burned), the initial burst of fertility was short lived, and some of the impoverished sandy soils began to drift. Windstorms would leave sand drifts across roads or clogging streams. "In the 1930s, the sand blew so hard there was a huge sand dune on Hwy 48," one man is quoted saying in a history of the York Regional Forest. "We made a trail through the bush to walk to school. You couldn't walk on the road with the sand whipping in your face."

This was the context in which Edmund John Zavitz began his job as Ontario's first provincial forester. Formerly productive forests had become sand "wastelands"—practically deserts—across the moraine, in Norfolk and Simcoe Counties, parts of eastern Ontario, and elsewhere. This was the foremost problem that Zavitz set out to solve in 1912. In his long career, he established modern forest fire prevention; he was influential in the creation of conservation reserves; and he created the agreement forest system that resulted in the York Regional Forest, Ganaraska Forest, and many others. But what he's best known for was reforesting southern Ontario, which earned him the informal title "Father of reforestation in Ontario."

The most obvious mark of Zavitz's legacy at Hollidge Tract is the red pine plantation that you find yourself in as soon as you enter the Tract. Here's a tree that seems out of place in southern Ontario, and yet red pine plantations are ubiquitous, often dating back more than 80 years. Red pine as a species has its roots primarily in thin soils over the bedrock of the Canadian Shield, in central and northern Ontario (though, as we see in Lambton Park, it's not quite that simple). Red pine plantations, however, can trace their origin story to Norfolk County and the Oak Ridges Moraine and Zavitz's tree-planting efforts.

Initially the most commonly planted trees in southern Ontario reforestation efforts were white pines, which were well adapted to the poor soils and exposed conditions of the wastelands. In some cases, white pines had been growing on the sites before they were cleared. But when the introduced disease, white pine blister rust, was found in Ontario in 1914, planting of white pine was all but abandoned in favour of red pine, which, Zavitz noted, "grows well on poor soil, has few enemies, and is valuable for timber purposes."

It's easy to dismiss the straight-row plantations of red pine as ecologically barren, compared to the rich shady hardwood forests that often naturally occur nearby. However, that would miss the point of the plantations, which was as a bridge from wastelands of blowing sand to, eventually, restored natural forests. The transition is accelerated by gradually harvesting the red pines to release the slow-growing hardwood trees beneath them, as York Regional Forest is now doing. This was probably Zavitz's intention when he planted them.

The expanding forests of southern Ontario did more than stabilize the soil, they also controlled flooding downstream. In a presentation in London, Ontario, in 1944, Zavitz remarked that "Rain falling on the forest floor does not run off suddenly, but it is taken up by the soil and stored for future use. Snows in winter are held under the forest cover and allowed to melt slowly ... forest cover tends to equalize the flow throughout the year by making the low flow stages higher, and the high stages lower."

This became the lived experience of residents on the Oak Ridges Moraine, who noted the sudden reappearance of streams and springs that

The perched yellow birch on the right started growing on the stump of a white pine, which might have been the parent tree of the white pine on the left.

had been lost for a generation or had only flowed seasonally. Long before the Oak Ridges Moraine was known as southern Ontario's metaphorical "rain barrel," towns on the moraine appreciated the importance of protecting a stable water supply, and this as much as anything drove many of the reforestation efforts in the first half of the 20th century.

This also basically sums up a core rationale for the Oak Ridges Moraine Conservation Plan, which protects the headwaters of many of the creeks of the Greater Toronto Area. I saw the effects of land transformation first-hand when I lived briefly in a rental home that backed onto Oshawa's Harmony Creek, technically in the Greenbelt but surrounded by suburbia. During a big rain, the creek would swell to spring flood levels, then within a day would subside to summer flows, with maybe a new piece of garbage lodged against the rocks. I was never sure if it was a good idea to let our then two-year-old son play on the sand bars that emerged when the waters sank. It may be too late for Harmony Creek, but the Greenbelt protects the headwaters and moderates the flow of many other creeks in the GTA.

But returning to Hollidge Tract, that's the story of the red pines that were planted around 1925 and are gradually being thinned to make way for maples and other hardwoods. You may even see some endangered butternuts on the edge of the red pines.

Before long you begin to descend through maple trees and into a wet forest, where yellow birch and cedar grow mixed into a hemlock forest. The hemlocks reach 120-to 140-years-old, though the oldest trees may be up to 160-years-old. One thing to look for are the very large old stumps, probably of white pine cut from this forest. Even when the stumps are mostly rotted away, the yellow birch and hemlock trees perched in the air memorialize the white pines that once stood here. At a guess, these white pines might have been cut around the same time that the red pines were planted on the hill above, or earlier.

There are some oldish sugar maples as you leave the wetland. There is also a forest of mature maple along the oak ridges trail and the connecting trail on the east side of the wetland, with scattered white pines (probably descendants of the giants that were logged from the wetland).

I like this site because it is hopeful. There are many forests in the Greenbelt that will become old growth in the lifetime of my children, or even in my lifetime. The Hollidge Tract reminds us that a forest can be restored after being seriously degraded. The red pines were planted to stabilize the sandy soil against erosion, but now, with a little help, the plantation is returning to a more natural forest.

Meanwhile the once-logged forest in the valley is returning to an old-growth state and is beautiful. This should make us treasure even more the few true undisturbed old-growth forests remaining in southern Ontario, while at the same time giving us a lot of hope for the future. But, like all our forests, invasive species are a persistent menace to the Hollidge Tract. A sign warning of hemlock woolly adelgid is a stark reminder that the status quo is killing our forests (see Tree Smart Trade in Thornton Bales, page 254).

The Oak Ridges Trail runs along the south side of the Hollidge Tract. If you were to hike the entire 275 km Oak Ridges Trail, it would also lead you past Peter's Woods at the east end, and Eaton Hall to the west, before finally joining with the Bruce Trail

Peter's Woods Provincial Nature Reserve

✤ What you'll like

This is the most intact, undisturbed forest remnant in Ontario's Greenbelt, with oak and maple trees reaching 300-to 400-years-old or more. It has all the hallmarks of old-growth forest, including logs, snags, old, and big trees.

✤ How to get there

By car – Peter's Woods is about 1.5 hours by car from Toronto, or an hour from Oshawa. There is plenty of parking except on very busy weekends, accessible from McDonald Road in Roseneath (44.1250, -78.0436).

By public transit – There are no convenient public transit options—the closest is probably Cobourg. The Oak Ridges Trail passes close to Peter's Woods and can be accessed from the Hwy 35/Hwy 115 Park and Ride, where there is a GO bus stop. However, there is little in the way of camping or accommodation between there and Peter's Woods, unless you can find a private rental close to the trail.

By bike – The Greenbelt cycle route runs right past the entrance to Peter's Woods on McDonald Road. There are outhouses at the parking lot.

✤ What to do

The nature trail is a short loop that can be walked in less than an hour. There are a couple of benches to rest and enjoy the view; take the time to admire the forest. On your walk, pay attention to the fern-rich understory and diverse bird community. This is a good place to learn more understory forest plants, and you may want to install the iNaturalist and Merlin apps on your phone if you don't already have them. Remember to sign the guestbook, as it helps secure funding for the trails (also, it's fun to see who else has been there).

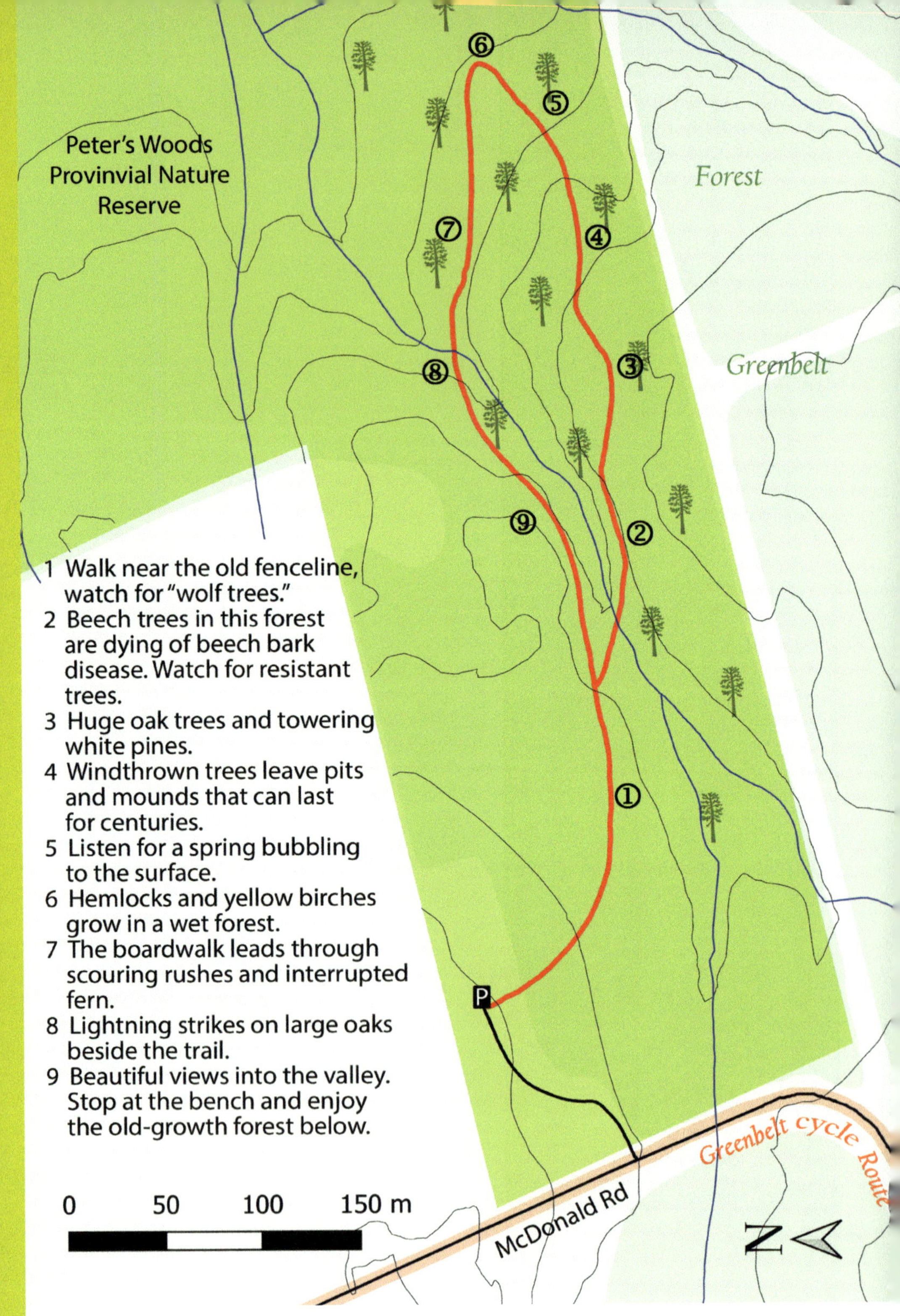
Peter's Woods
Provinvial Nature
Reserve
Forest
Greenbelt
Greenbelt cycle Route
McDonald Rd
P
1 Walk near the old fenceline, watch for "wolf trees."
2 Beech trees in this forest are dying of beech bark disease. Watch for resistant trees.
3 Huge oak trees and towering white pines.
4 Windthrown trees leave pits and mounds that can last for centuries.
5 Listen for a spring bubbling to the surface.
6 Hemlocks and yellow birches grow in a wet forest.
7 The boardwalk leads through scouring rushes and interrupted fern.
8 Lightning strikes on large oaks beside the trail.
9 Beautiful views into the valley. Stop at the bench and enjoy the old-growth forest below.
0
50
100
150 m
N

✣ Learn more

Peter's Woods is the only untouched pre-settlement forest on the Oak Ridges Moraine, with trees dating back to at least the 1600s. This makes it a very special place, where you can see the intact structure and processes of the forest. Dead trees are abundant, both as standing snags and fallen logs in all stages of decay. There's a rich understory of ferns, scouring rush, saplings, and shrubs of all descriptions. And the trees are old. White oaks and maples reach at least 400-years-old, with estimated ages for both over 460 years (approaching the longevity of these species). A few centuries ago, a windstorm or fire killed part of the forest and allowed white pines to start growing. These trees are now over 280-years-old and reach 37 metres (11 storeys) tall.

I'm walking with local naturalist Amy Quinn, and as soon as we walk into the forest, she spots the egg cases of gypsy moth on trees and begins scraping them off. This was the first sign of something that quickly became clear to me: Quinn acts as a steward of Peter's Woods. "Now I'll have to come back for this," she says, as she drops some egg cases into a bag. "It's a good thing I'm retired." Recently she encountered a man tearing logs apart and rolling them over to photograph salamanders in the forest. Anyone who understands how unique Peter's Woods is would find it disturbing, but this clearly bothers Quinn on a deeper level.

"You have to understand," she says, "I've been watching these logs decay for years. Peter's Woods has been the one constant in my life." Quinn grew up living down the road from the forest, which at the time was called McDonald Woods. She recalls how her mother would pack a picnic basket and the whole family would walk a mile up the road. The children were not even allowed to sit down as their father would recount the story of McDonald Woods. As he told it, the McDonald family had to pay a fine to the Crown because they refused to cut the trees in the woodlot. And there's no doubt the family left it largely alone, even leaving

This disease-resistant beech tree just off the trail says FU to beech bark disease.

most of the large white pines that were very valuable at the time. Later, when the family decided to sell the property, they had offers to buy the land for the value of the lumber on it, but preferred to sell it to Peter Schultz, who told them he'd turn it into a nature reserve. "They were happy with that," Amy Quinn tells me.

Initially, we're walking along through an old field that has grown into a forest of birch and poplar over the past half-century or so. As the trail turns, it skirts the edge of the young forest on the left, while on the right are large old trees that were once at the forest edge. These "wolf trees" have characteristics of having grown in the open, with large low-growing branches or old branch knots where shaded branches have died but left their mark. The real magic begins in the valley after the trail crosses the stream on a small bridge. This part of the forest is all but untouched, and some of the oaks and maples found here have lived for over 400 years. The oldest trees are typically not the largest trees; watch instead for characteristics like bark balding, and large twisty branches high on the tree. Stand on the bridge and look around; you'll probably see some trees that fit the description. You'll also see some big trees, especially oaks.

As you climb the slope away from the creek, you'll reach post #1. When this post was installed, it was beside a healthy beech tree. When the trail guide was last revised, the beech tree had a white waxy scale insect and a red fungus growing on the bark. Now the beech is dead and fallen over beside the post. This is the progress of beech bark disease (see Bronte Creek, page 139, to learn more). Fortunately, just a little further down the trail on the right is a healthy beech tree that is resistant to the beech scale. Roughly one or two percent of beech trees usually have this resistance. Trees like this are very important; every seed that it produces has the potential to be part of the next generation of resistant, healthy beech trees, with their beautiful smooth grey bark.

As you continue along the trail, you'll pass maple and oak trees with signs of old age, then you'll start seeing white pines towering among them. The oaks and pines found here suggest that something has disturbed this forest in the past, either wind or fire. This was hundreds of years ago so it's hard to be sure either way, though pine and oak hint at fire. Certainly, wind has been and is still a force in this forest. You'll pass some impressive windthrown trees, especially a long curved red oak that blew down alongside the trail, taking a lot of soil with it. Look closely at the forest floor as you go down the hill and you'll see it is often very uneven, with large mounds where tree roots lifted up a lot of soil, and shallow pits where the tree once stood. Some of them have no hint left of the tree that once fell, these are centuries old. In fact, this pit and mound topography can persist for over a thousand years after a tree falls! Peter's Woods has clearly been an old-growth forest for a long time.

As we walk down the hill, Quinn draws my attention to the sound of running water—a natural spring where a small stream suddenly appears out of the ground with a cheerful bubbling noise. "The drumlins around here are just full of water," she says—a reminder that we are on the Oak Ridges Moraine, Ontario's "rain barrel" (read more in the introduction, page 17). Another sign that groundwater is seeping to the surface are moisture-loving plants like interrupted and sensitive ferns, as well as scouring rushes that suddenly become abundant. These tall leafless stalks, loaded with silica, are actually a type of horsetail that thrives in wet conditions.

As you round the bend in the trail, you'll find a hemlock forest to your right; hemlocks also thrive in moist soils, often growing alongside streams. The trail continues along a boardwalk surrounded by scouring rush. Watch for the interrupted ferns near the end of the boardwalk. All of the trail maintenance in this forest is done by the volunteers of the Willow Beach

Tree cavities are habitat for wildlife of all kinds ....

Field Naturalists. The stainless-steel wire mesh that provides traction on the boardwalk was added by Karen Drew, who coordinates trail maintenance. She got the idea in New Zealand where it's common. Every trail in Peter's Woods leads back to the Willow Beach Field Naturalists. Peter Schultz (who bought the land) was a founding member of the naturalists, and the club has taken a lead in its management ever since.

After you cross the second bridge, look for a lightning strike curving up a red oak on your right. The tree has been clinging to life for many years, but may soon succumb to the damage. On the other side of the trail, another oak that was struck by lightning has nearly healed over the scar. Enjoy views into the valley as you continue your walk along the ridge back toward your car (or bicycle). You might even want to hike the loop a second time; you're sure to notice new wonders along the way.

Index

A striped sweat bee on New England aster.

References and Further Reading

Ancient Forest Exploration & Research. https://www.ancientforest.org/

Bacher, J. (2011). 2 Billion Trees and Counting: The Legacy of Edmund Zavitz. Dundurn Press.

Banks, P. B., & Bryant, J. V. (2007). Four-legged friend or foe? Dog walking displaces native birds from natural areas. Biology Letters, 3(6), 611–613. https://doi.org/10.1098/RSBL.2007.0374

Caldwell, W., Epp, S., Wan, X., Singer, R., Drake, E., & Sousa, E. C. (2022). Farmland Preservation and Urban Expansion: Case Study of Southern Ontario, Canada. Frontiers in Sustainable Food Systems, 6 (February), 1–17. https://doi.org/10.3389/fsufs.2022.777816

Cary Institute of Ecosystem Studies. Tree-SMART Trade | Cary Institute of Ecosystem Studies. http://www.caryinstitute.org/science-program/research-projects/tree-smart-trade

Cheskey, E. (2003). Twelve Mile Creek Headwaters Important Bird Area. http://www.ibacanada.ca/documents/conservationplans/ontwelvemilecreekheadwater.pdf

Colpitts, G. W. (2017). The Reconstructed Longhouse and Environmental History. Network in Canadian History & Environment (NICHE). https://niche-canada.org/2017/06/19/the-reconstructed-longhouse-and-e-history/

David Suzuki Foundation and Ontario Nature. (2011). Biodiversity in Ontario's Greenbelt. https://ontarionature.org/wp-content/uploads/2017/10/REPORT-GB_Habitat-Dec2011.pdf

Davies, E., Dong, A., Berka, C., Scrivener, P., Taylor, D., & Smith, S. M. (2018). The Toronto Ravines Study: 1977-2017 Long-term Changes in the Biodiversity and Ecological Integrity of Toronto's Ravines. https://torontoravinesdotorg.files.wordpress.com/2018/09/toronto-ravines-study-1977-to-2017-with-component-studies.pdf

Davis, M. B. (Ed.). (1996). Eastern Old-Growth Forests: Prospects for Rediscovery and Recovery. Island Press.

Eaton, F. M. (1956). Memory's wall. Clarke, Irwin & Company.

Gaige, M. (2011). A place for wolf trees. Northern Woodlands, Spring, 28–32. https://northernwoodlands.org/articles/article/a-place-for-wolf-trees

Garratt, J. E. Nature Reserve on the City's Edge. https://www.kobo.com/ca/en/ebook/nature-reserve-on-the-city-s-edge

Gerber, R. E., & Howard, K. (2002). Hydrogeology of the Oak Ridges Moraine aquifer system: implications for protection and management from the Duffins Creek watershed. Can. J. Earth Sci, 39, 1333–1348. https://doi.org/10.1139/E02-058

Grindrod, J. (2018). Outskirts: Living life on the edge of the Green Belt. Sceptre.

Henry, M. Beech bark disease resistance. http://www.oldgrowth.ca/wp-content/uploads/Beech-Bark-Disease-Resistance.pdf

Henry, M., & Quinby, P. (2022). Ontario's old-growth forests 2nd edition. Fitzhenry and Whiteside.

Jennings, N. (2018). Lightfoot. Penguin Canada.

Johnson, L. (2017). 100 Easy-to-Grow Native Plants for Canadian Gardens. Douglas & McIntyre.

Johnson, L. (2023). A Northern Gardener's Guide to Native Plants and Pollinators. Island Press.

Karim Tiro. (2018). Wither the salmon? Network in Canadian History & Environment (NICHE). https://niche-canada.org/2018/07/23/whither-the-salmon/

Kelly, P. E., & Larson, D. W. (2007). The Last Stand: A Journey Through the Ancient Cliff-Face Forest of the Niagara Escarpment. Dundurn Press.

Kershner, B. (2004). Old Growth Forest Survey of Eastern Niagara Peninsula Phase 2/ Final Report. http://www.nativetreesociety.org/specialreports/niagara/Niagara_peninsula_old_growth_01.pdf

Kershner, B., & Leverett, R. (2004). The Sierra Club guide to the ancient forests of the northeast. Sierra Club Books. https://archive.org/details/sierraclubguideto0bruc

Leopold, A. (1949). A Sand County Almanac.

Leung, B., Lodge, D. M., Finnoff, D., Shogren, J. F., Lewis, M. a, & Lamberti, G. (2002). An ounce of prevention or a pound of cure: Bioeconomic risk analysis of invasive species. Proceedings. Biological Sciences / The Royal Society, 269(1508), 2407–2413. https://doi.org/10.1098/rspb.2002.2179

Lovett, G. M., Weiss, M., Liebhold, A. M., Holmes, T. P., Leung, B., Lambert, K. F., Orwig, D. A., Campbell, F. T., Rosenthal, J., McCullough, D. G., Wildova, R., Ayres, M. P., Canham, C. D., Foster, D. R., La Deau, S. L., & Weldy, T. (2016). Nonnative forest insects and pathogens in the United States: Impacts and policy options. Ecological Applications, 26(5), 1437–1455. https://doi.org/10.1890/15-1176

Luoma, J. (2006). The hidden forest: the biography of an ecosystem. OSU Press.

Luyssaert, S., Schulze, E.-D., Börner, A., Knohl, A., Hessenmöller, D., Law, B. E., Ciais, P., & Grace, J. (2008). Old-growth forests as global carbon sinks. Nature, 455(7210), 213–215. https://doi.org/10.1038/nature07276

MacGregor, R., Haxton, T. M., Greig, L. A., Casselman, J. M., Dettmers, J. M., Allen, W. A., Oliver, D. G., & McDermott, L. (2012). Demise of American Eel in the Upper St. Lawrence River, Lake Ontario, Ottawa River and Associated Watersheds: Implications of Regional Cumulative Effects. American Fisheries Society Symposium, 78, 1–40. http://www.ontarioriversalliance.ca/wp-content/uploads/2015/06/macgregor_cumulative-effects_finalfinal.pdf

Martin, N. D., & Martin, N. M. (2009). Biotic forest communities of Ontario (4th ed.). Commonwealth Research.

Mississaugas of the Credit First Nation. https://mncfn.ca/

Mitchell, A. (2023). The Anthropocene is here — and tiny Crawford Lake has been chosen as the global ground zero | Canadian Geographic. Canadian Geographic. https://canadiangeographic.ca/articles/the-anthropocene-is-here-and-tiny-crawford-lake-has-been-chosen-as-the-global-ground-zero/

North American Native Plant Society. https://nanps.org/

Ontario's old-growth forests: Tall pines, 1000 year-old cedars, and old forests in your local park. https://www.oldgrowth.ca

Ontario's oldest trees. https://www.oldgrowth.ca/oldtrees/

ORTA. (2021). Oak Ridges Moraine Trail guidebook (7th edition). Oak Ridges Trail Association. https://www.oakridgestrail.org/store/

Pederson, N. (2010). External Characteristics of Old Trees in the Eastern Deciduous Forest. Natural Areas Journal, 30(4), 396–407. https://doi.org/10.3375/043.030.0405

Riley, J. L. (2013). The once and future Great Lakes country: and ecological history. McGill-Queen's University Press.

Roy, B. A., Alexander, H. M., Davidson, J., Campbell, F. T., Burdon, J. J., Sniezko, R., & Brasier, C. (2014). Increasing forest loss worldwide from invasive pests requires new trade regulations. Frontiers in Ecology and the Environment, 12(8), 457–465. https://doi.org/10.1890/130240

Sandberg, L. A., Wekerle, G. R., & Gilbert, L. (2013). The oak ridges moraine battles: Development, sprawl, and nature conservation in the Toronto region. University of Toronto Press.

Sauriol, C. (1981). Remembering the Don: A Rare Record of Earlier Times Within the Don River Valley. Consolidated Amethyst Communications.

Sauriol, C. (1992). Trails of the Don. Hemlock Press.

Suffling, R., Evans, M., & Perera, A. (2003). Presettlement forest in southern Ontario: Ecosystems measured through a cultural prism. Forestry Chronicle, 79(3), 485–501. https://doi.org/10.5558/tfc79485-3

Tallamy, D. W. (2004). Do alien plants reduce insect biomass? In Conservation Biology (Vol. 18, Issue 6). https://doi.org/10.1111/j.1523-1739.2004.00512.x

Tallamy, D. W. (2009). Bringing nature home : how you can sustain wildlife with native plants. Timber Press.

Tallamy, D. W. (2019). Nature's best hope: a new approach to conservation that starts in your yard. Timber Press

The Alliance for a Liveable Ontario. https://www.liveableontario.ca/

Thoms, J. M. (2004). Ojibwa fishing grounds : a history of Ontario fisheries law, science, and the sportsmen's challenge to Aboriginal treaty rights, 1650-1900. University of British Columbia Library. https://doi.org/10.14288/1.0091924

Turner, G. (2015). The Toronto Carrying Place: Rediscovering Toronto's most ancient trail. Dundurn Press.

Tyson, D. E. (2017). Trail to the Bruce: the story of the building of the Bruce Trail. Tellwell Publishing. https://brucetrail.org/product/trail-to-the-bruce-paperback/

Wessels, T. (1997). Reading the forested landscape. The Countryman Press.

MIKE'S FAVOURITE NATIVE PLANTS

Native plant gardening is easy and fun, but you might not know where to begin. I don't recommend tearing out your lawn and planting a prairie; instead start with smaller beds and experiment with different groups of plants, then expand from there. Below is a list of some of my favourite plants grouped by habitat; the plants in each group will tend to grow well together.

You can create a simple rain garden by digging a shallow hole or basin near your downspout which will fill with water each time it rains. You can make a tiny green roof atop a shed and see which species love to grow there. Have fun with it!

Ground covers
Wild ginger
Wood violet *(Viola sororia)*

Green roof or dry rock garden
Calamint
Early saxifrage
Wild columbine

Tall low-maintenance sun
Bee-balm
Canada goldenrod/goldenrod species
Heart-leaved aster
New-England aster

Shade garden
Bloodroot
Bottlebrush grass
Canada anemone
Lady fern
Ostrich fern (fiddlehead)
Wild ginger
Zigzag goldenrod

Rain garden
Blue-flag iris
Cardinal flower
Joe pye weed
Swamp milkweed

Prairie
Black-eyed Susan
Butterfly milkweed
Canada wild rye
Dense blazing star
Indian grass
Little bluestem

Shrubs
Elderberry
Nannyberry
Pagoda dogwood
Serviceberry/Amelanchier species